12 Gauge Shotkids

The Perfect Guide to Handling Baby Mama Drama

Rodney L. Clark Jr.

Soulja Soulja

Copyright © 2016 R3D Books

All rights reserved.

ISBN: **0692640819**

ISBN-13: **978-0692640814**

DEDICATION

This book is dedicated to all of the children worldwide that suffer from co-parent drama. The ones that have to quietly suffer from a parent either not wanting to be in their lives or have been forced out of their lives by the other parent. In loving memory of Dymond Clark. This book is also dedicated to my son Dyshawn Young, who also is a child that has been taken out of the life of the only father he has ever known due to senseless players of this very old game that produces no winners in the end.

CONTENTS

	Words From The Author	i
1	Choose Wisely	1
2	Loving and Respecting the Mother of Your Child	Pg 12
3	When the Relationship Can't Work	Pg 23
4	Loving Your Children More Than You Hate Their Mother	Pg 32
5	Establishing Paternity and Visitation	Pg 42
6	Dealing With the Court System	Pg 53
7	Why Does She Hate Me	Pg 64
8	Controlling Your Anger and Her Bitterness	Pg 74
9	Comforting the Kids During These Trying Times	Pg 87
10	Consequences for the 'Bad Parent'	Pg 99

Words from the Author

It is my honor and my duty to present to the world this book that I have respectively titled '12 Gauge Shotkids.' It has been my focus for at least seven years now to promote effective parenting in our young adults that have been suffering from an ongoing war between co-parents. As a father of three children, I have enjoyed raising my children to the best of my ability. They are my motivation if I've never had the proper motivation before. They keep me determined. I look forward to tomorrow because of them. I strive to do better for them. Being a parent is the greatest responsibility that I will ever have in life and I always find a way to find satisfaction in it and cherish it. I don't brag about being the best father in the world or try to portray to the world that I'm doing something so extraordinary. I'm doing exactly what I'm supposed to be doing if I was going to bring children in this world. I don't deserve a trophy or a medal for what I committed myself to do. I don't even deserve all of the kudos that committed fathers get nowadays for simply doing what they are supposed to be doing as much as the mother is. You don't hear people praising mothers for being in their children's lives, but for fathers it has somehow turned into an act worthy of recognition. This is a problem, and a big one at that.

At the age of twenty-one, I had my very first child who also suffered from heart disease. She took nine to ten medicines around the clock and needed very much attention, love, and care. She spent long periods in the hospital and I couldn't help but to man up and be the best father I could be in order to see to it that my child was well taken care of and made it back home. This never happened though. She later died from the heart disease at the age of eleven months. It was something that I had never thought that I would experience in this life. I never thought that I would lose my child to death before me. Even after her diagnosis I didn't think anything about actually losing her. With those thoughts never entering my mind, I must admit that I was slightly neglectful in caring for her. I still behaved as if I had a perfectly normal baby, and she was far from that. She was sick and I was eventually going to lose her. After her death all that I could think about was my own mother telling me that I needed to pay more attention to her because we never know when we can lose these babies. Those words stick to me to this day. From that point on I

Soulja Soulja

never saw myself not taking full responsibility in my children's lives. I knew that they needed me and I definitely couldn't see myself losing another one or not being there for any of them. I also had it in my own mind that I never wanted to have multiple children because I could lessen my chances of that ever happening to me again. I also wondered why we would even want to bring children into a world that is so cruel and evil anyway. I wondered why we would bring children into a world without being able to know if we can be fully responsible for them, love them fully, and allow them to have a mother and a father together.

Nothing ever made me more worried than to think that I would have children that would grow up in a single family household. I hated the thought of my children possibly being shuffled from house to house, only seeing me on weekends, or even worse their mother taking them from me. If I was ever able to foresee this in mine and my children's future I would have never had one child. That has always been a nightmare to me. And sadly this has become my reality and the reality of many other mothers and fathers. I even thought at one point that I had my co-parent all figured out while we were together and creating life together. I was with her for plenty of years. She would never do these things to me, her, or our family. I could even settle with a breakup, knowing that things may not always work out the way we initially saw, but I never wanted to feel that she would take my children from me, deny me parenting time, force me into the court system, grow what seems like an everlasting hatred and envy for me, turn on me, or even worse damage the minds or stop taking the well being of our children seriously. All of that happened though from a woman that once loved the very ground that I stood on. There was nothing that I could do about it but be determined that no one was going to force me out of my kid's lives and that I was going to fight for them in any way that I needed to and for however long that it took. One thing that I wasn't going to do is give up on my children. I had been through too much to ever let one person do that to me because I was going to be the one that had to live with the consequences of that in the end. My very first daughter had died. No more than eight months later we welcomed in another little girl that seemed to be like a reincarnation of what we just lost. We had a little boy that was conceived during a

12 Gauge Shotkids

year-long separation and was told that he possibly wasn't mine but I accepted him in my life as his father since no one else would step up. So I had three, went down to two, and as soon as we separated for good her and her parents took the little boy from my life. I went down to one child. So maybe you can see how I've lost so much dealing with children; I have no choice but to be everything to the one little girl that I have that can't be denied or taken from me.

Throughout the whole ordeal I had to learn patience, self-control, and how to deal with hurt. It hurts badly when someone takes your child from you, but you can't show it, you have to fight. It's not easy to have to argue, fuss, and fight all of the time just to be in your child's life, especially when it wasn't like this before. But you have to deal with it and strategize to make things better. It takes so much time and there is no specific timeframe on when things will change. All that I know is that when there is drama it takes a bigger person to start putting out the fire. I chose to be that bigger person. And once I did things started to change. After five long years of back and forth bickering and difficulties, court appearances, missed holidays, birthdays, and overall parenting time, I now have custody of that one daughter that I've fought so hard for. I was let back into my son's life for about a good year, but only to have him taken from me again. He's not my biological child so I can't fight for him, but I love him dearly and have since the day he was born. I just hold on to the fact that he knows exactly who I am and he has to get older one day. He will come back to me. Overall I just want people to know that this is an old game being played by new players. The new players aren't even trying to play the game any different than it's already been played in the past. The game is foolish and there are no winners in the end. Everybody loses, especially the children. If you love your mother and father, or if you didn't get that opportunity to love either one for whatever reasons but would have loved to love them, think about your own child that you may be hurting by not giving them the chance to love both of their creators equally. Things happen and relationships change, but the love for your children should always remain strong.

For some reason it has become a fad to be a single parent. But that is far from cool, and it usually forces our children to live in the struggle that they shouldn't even need to be in. Nowadays there are mothers bragging about being daddy too. True enough, she may be the breadwinner, or the handywoman, or the supporter that dad would and should be, but a mother could never be what a father is to a child. A mother has a much

Soulja Soulja

different impact on a child than a father would. So mothers should never claim to be fathers too. It just isn't true. She would know the difference if that child's father were actually there. And a lot of the time these mothers are the main reason that the fathers that they complain about so much aren't there. She forced him out just to dog him later without explaining to the world her role in his absence. None of it is acceptable, but it is our reality and it needs to change ASAP. This is a state of emergency and the drama is destroying our children's minds, their futures, and their overall progression. We are creating monsters that are going to create a destructive world all because we can't get along and raise them responsibly while they are still children. There is a void in these children as they grow up without a certain parent and history has proven that they are going to fill it somehow, and it's not always going to be in a good way. So we need to start now by controlling our anger, our moods, our feelings, our ways, our judgment, and our attitude and focus on doing better for our children. You may think that it doesn't start with you until you see how being positive will have your children touching many others in a positive way, and by you being negative how many people they will touch in a negative way. We can change this cycle one household at a time. Once we start realizing this as a problem and stop encouraging co-parents to attack one another, we will start to see a change in our society. Even if you don't care so much about society, start to care about your own household and the well being of your children and the world that surrounds you will change on its own. God bless your family.

12 Gauge Shotkids

1 CHOOSE WISELY

The biggest mistake that we make as men is not carefully screening the women/ or girls that we get ourselves involved with. Being too busy trying to satisfy our sexual desires and please our ego's are the main reasons why we end up with no good mothers for our children.

It's not really the fact that the woman is no good altogether; it's the fact that she isn't good for you, and who you are, and what you are trying to do in your life. We make irreversible damages by catering to our fantasies, seeing and getting the attention of thrill seekers, and mistaking first impressions for lasting impressions. We tend to take far less time than what is needed when choosing the mother for our children. That is even when we weren't necessarily choosing, but still wound up with someone that we share a child or children with.

Soulja Soulja

When you do decide to create a family, you need to make sure that you don't create a family that you don't intend to care for and love. This is important, especially during the screening process. It will help you pay more attention to the qualities and characteristics of the potential mother for your children. When a man decides to create a family he should be focused on what type of man he wants to be to that family. You will find yourself being much less reckless when encountering women if you have a focus on what kind of family you desire. Truthfully, all people show what type of person they really are during the first weeks of getting to know them; we just pay more attention to what it is that we want from them more than we pay attention to what kind of person they truly are. Knowing the family that you desire to create is the key to understanding the kind of family that you don't want. So once someone displays behaviors and characteristics that you won't allow in your life you will be faster to get away.

You will also find that you will care so much more for that family's well being. You will care so much more for the mother of your children. You will protect yourself from the mistakes of having unwanted children. You will continue to strive to be a better man and father to a family that you have all intentions on being there for. Men who make the mistake of having too many flings and involving themselves with several different women for selfish needs or sexual purposes wind up with the unwanted children that they didn't mentally prepare themselves for. This increases the chances of most of these men skipping out on the mother and the child. When you don't really know the mother of your child you have a much harder time understanding the ways and the behaviors of the child you created. Men who have no intentions on caring for the family that they created usually ends up dealing with a distant relationship with one or more of their kids if they do decide to stick around in some kind of way. The relationship between a mother and a father who moved to co-parenting with each other way too fast only creates mass confusion and frustration when attempting to stay together due to the lack of thorough knowledge of one another, which usually leads to an even faster break down then break up. It becomes easy for the two

12 Gauge Shotkids

to disagree on just about everything. Personal relationship issues and the children all of a suddenly become a bonus issue. The child then becomes caught up in the wraths of combative and angry parents that rarely can get along, even for the sake of simply raising the child up in stable and providing environments.

A real man that creates a family pledges to care for them whether he is with the mother or not. He realizes that the well being of the family is based off of the well being of both the mother and father. He wants the mother to do well with or without him. This is how a family stays healthy even in the absence of another parent. Children love to see their parents get along. A father that stops caring for the family only sets himself up for problems in the future. You should never flip around making babies with several women just because you want several children or control of particular women that you have encounters with. It starts with understanding the family that you desire and the type of woman that you want to share that blessing with. Otherwise you are setting yourself up for all of the oldest games being played every day by the newest players. And ultimately the family loses in the beginning and in the end. This is why we have a generation now full of single mothers and fathers, deadbeat dads and moms, and distracted and troublesome children. It mostly resulted from the creation of a family created from all of the wrong reasoning and choices.

I can remember being very young and always listening to my mother talk to me about so many different things that dealt with life. Although I don't recall the actual words she said anymore, the impact that she was installing in her child was slowly building the right from wrong aspect that she knew would guide me through challenging roads that my life may lead me through. I didn't need to remember what it was that she said more than I needed to understand what it was that she was installing in me. She was helping to build my character. Your character will always remain. Once I became a teenager, and later an adult, I was able to control what I allowed her to install in me more than I could as a child. I guess this is why it is important for a parent to shape their children

Soulja Soulja

while they are very young, because the fact that after a child can control what your impact on them is once they get older it makes it less of a chance of effectively getting anything through to them. It's definitely not impossible, but chances decrease drastically. As a child you listened to everything she had to say. You absorbed all of it. Once you got older you only listened to and absorbed what you wanted to. If you heard what you didn't want to hear you could discard it. No matter what went in one ear and out the other, or what remained, mama was usually right. Why would she be interested in telling you anything wrong? What you can count on with most mother and son relationships, she will always be able to school you on women. Your mother will be very critical of the women that you bring around, whether openly or indirect. Your mother can tell what type of woman is right for her son. I haven't quite figured out the science on it, but it seems that most likely a man will have a strong attraction to women that are different than his mother, and will still find himself only settling with a woman that is so similar to his mother. He hates for his mother to downplay the women he is really attracted to and lust over, but can't help but notice that she was right once none of them seemed to work out. It's almost like she can look at whoever it is that you are with and can tell all the reasons you are with her. She knows that once you've fulfilled your agenda with her that ya'll relationship will be history. Maybe she knows what she has installed in you won't allow you to have longevity with someone that has the characteristics and behaviors that particular woman displays. Plus she knows what type of person you are as well. She knows what you can and can't handle, and will or won't put up with. She knows your likenesses as her own child. She may be open or indirect, but she is always watching as it slowly falls apart. If she is open, it is a very good idea to at least consider her thoughts. This mainly applies to men that have mothers that want to see them with someone and being happy with them. A mother's first impression of the woman is usually an unbiased and far different impression than yours would be. She usually won't see what you see. A mother knows your heart better than anyone and will tell you like it is. As a man you will most likely still give it a chance despite what mom says, but be prepared to face the truths

12 Gauge Shotkids

behind her warnings. She may have her initial doubts and still eventually grow a love or a tolerance for the lady. She is going to respect who has your heart. But she can still like someone and at the same time have that feeling that she isn't going to be right for her child.

Mothers know best in many of these cases. You don't have to listen, but you will eventually see what it is that they are saying. The one out of a hundred that she accepts and/or embraces is usually the keeper. It all depends on how you treat her and accept her too. Mothers definitely can be wrong too, but their insights are gold. A lot of us have spent our lives wasting what our mothers told us just to wind up paying for it later. This works the same when it comes to the women that we think we will spend our lives with. Mother will be by our side regardless, but think about all that she has to watch us put ourselves through, and her too, if we don't heed to her warning signs and choose the wrong person. We save ourselves a lot of trouble and headache by at least taking note of and observing what she sees in our potential life partner.

Another important factor to consider is does she have the ability to take care for herself? Can she provide her own self with the basic things that an adult needs to survive? Will she work a job? Does she still need too much assistance from her parents? Does she have a car? Will she break you financially? If you were to build anything with her and lost it all on your end, would she be able and willing to step up and back you up?

Again, we have to get past looks and desires. We have to get past lusting. We have to really stare at what type of person we are dealing with. Initially, everyone has all the right words to get the others attention, but do the words match the action? Is what she says really what you see? Getting caught up in words and feelings can definitely lead to making the mistake of going too far with the wrong woman. If she can't take care of herself, how do you expect her to take care of your children? How can she be any kind of woman that you need her to be for you? It's not a crime for a young woman to lack adult skills, but it is disastrous to think it is

Soulja Soulja

any kind of good idea to make this premature woman a mother. If anything, do your best to train her right if this happens to be the woman you want to be with. Help her see what it takes to be an adult and put her to the test. You would be surprised to see how unprepared most women are when handling issues and responsibilities on an adult level, especially the ones that never had to fend for themselves much. Don't be fooled by her age either. Just because they are over eighteen or twenty one still doesn't make a person an adult, and definitely not a responsible one at that. You should pay attention to action because you will be misled by words.

Once you can see how her parents raised her and how they influence her life today, you will have a better understanding of where her maturity level is. Looking at the examples that her parents installed in her will show you what she has been exposed to, and may likely wind up mimicking. If she is lazy, or has reckless immediate family, she may lean more towards that life. Why not? It has been installed in her that this is the way to live. If her parents or immediate family are well educated and employed, naturally she may lean more toward those influences as well. Some women are resentful and/or traumatized by abusive natures, while others come from good, steady backgrounds and still don't pursue further education and have no problem with being unemployed most of the time. When you take it easy and pay attention to her, she will show you everything that you need to know. Take words much lighter than you would take their actions. With time everyone has to show their true self.

A mature woman that can take care of herself is the type of mother you should be expecting to have your children. This is the type of woman that you should make a mistake with if you were going to make a mistake. Trust me, the two will save you years of hurt and pain. A mature woman will focus on what is healthy for the family. An immature woman will hurt the family some kind of childish and ridiculous way. A mature woman will work with you if the relationship fails. An immature woman will do everything in her power to attack you and hope for your downfalls. A mature woman

12 Gauge Shotkids

will have no interest in playing games. An immature woman conspires to play games with your mind and your children. If she can't take care of herself you will find yourself taking care of her every need for however long the relationship lasts. If and when it does fail you can never depend on her to provide stable housing and care for your children. She has been so used to being taken care of that when she is forced to do it on her own she will fail miserably. You would much rather her go through these types of life battles without having your children. You should always remember that whatever she goes through the children go through as well. Taking the time to find that mature woman/mother is priceless. It won't cost your future, break your pockets, or cost your children and their futures the same that it will with those that are premature to life.

Basically, a mature woman/mother for your children is a partner. Your intentions should be to make her your partner. You don't want a super dependent, crybaby little girl. You can have only one baby by her and still feel as though you are raising two kids. This is a terrible situation for a man. It also causes you to give up on the family much faster. You don't have someone that can keep up with your pace. If you fall, it all falls down. Whatever decisions you make it's always yes-yes and not much valuable feedback. The relationship lacks the necessary communication to make it strong.

You don't need all of that though. All of these things come along with not choosing wisely. And when you involve kids into the equation you find yourself trapped. You really need someone that is and can be a partner. She needs to be able to effectively communicate with you and not be afraid to disagree. When you find yourself falling down you need her to be able to catch you and assist you with bringing the household and/or relationship back together. You need her to have goals and ideas. She needs to represent you correctly, and you need to do the same with her.

Ambitious men are never sleep on the next venture or idea. This type of man needs someone who can bring light to his eyes. A brilliant idea with a good, steady partnership can change the course of a relationship drastically. It can change financial situations and bring about moments that can become highlights of your relationship. She can come up with easier ways to carry out goals. She can come up with more ideas. She can handle tasks that you don't wish to handle. She can be your motivation, your encouragement; she can be the reason for success. A good partnership between couples is the perfect transition from traditional ways of coupling. It's better when ya'll find something to do to make the relationship more fun and more interesting. This is how families create businesses and wealth that their children can later benefit from. This is how you take your lady's attention from normal temptations and give her something way more serious and beneficial to focus on. What could another guy do for her by just talking game in her ear when her man at home is already an innovator and showing her how to become a productive entrepreneur? You have to examine the benefits of making your woman your partner. Too many idle people in relationships want to discover further what it is that everyone else is doing so interesting.

It's just as bad to have an uninvolved woman on your team as it is to be a man that doesn't involve his woman in what he does. She can't be a partner if she isn't in on what you do. Of course, she probably can't be involved with everything that goes on, but you should be able to find her something to do. This makes her feel special and may open her mind up on ways to make your life better. Don't underestimate her no matter what. Even if you already have a team, she can still be a valuable member that you can trust with intelligence that others don't know yet. She can approve or disapprove what you intend to share with others. She can give you insight on plenty that haven't even come to your mind yet.

There is always a place for a good partner. It's so much better than not ever seeing eye to eye with someone you are committed to. It's better than someone that never shares with you what is on their mind; you are with someone that you always have to guess about. When dealing with the kids, disagreements come to a peaceful

12 Gauge Shotkids

resolution, as the two can be more level-headed and can better try to understand one another. The main thing is that the partners grow together. This is very important to the children and their upbringing. Two people that are just together for the sake of the kids and are doing their own thing on the side usually just grow apart. Their households suffer more chaos and confusion. Their kids are forced to take sides. Each is more prone to let outsiders into their ears, thus, destroying whatever was built in the first place.

Work on getting a mature woman that is also a partner and makes your life so much better and easier. It won't be perfect, but it can be so much more worthwhile. You do not need sneaky and lying women. Once you see sneakiness and constantly hear lies those aren't good signs of building a strong relationship. Sneaky women can be some of the worse ones to deal with. They are the ones with all of the right words, but none of the action to match the words. In order to be themselves they have to sneak and do it. At least this is what they feel they need to do.

A sneaky woman can really make your life miserable. What comes along with being sneaky is dishonesty. You always find yourself spinning in circles trying to figure out what it is that they are up to. A sneaky woman will pull fast ones on you every chance she gets once she learns how to catch you with your guard down. She will cheat on you with other men. She will venture to places she knows she shouldn't be. She will keep you wondering and guessing. Ultimately, the main reason you don't want to get yourself involved with a sneaky woman is because she will never learn how to let you in her world the way that you need to be.

The sneaky woman is only out for self. She can't care about you or your feelings, or the relationship, the way that she should. She can't be everything that you need her to be. Her agendas are her own and she doesn't want you fishing around or trying to decipher what it is that she is about and what she does. She can be poisonous. You can never get very far with sneaky women if you are the type that is intelligent enough to know when you are being

Soulja Soulja

played. It's not very hard to notice when she is hiding things from you. It is mainly up to you to stop turning a blind eye to her ways. Once you have asked and learned enough about her ethical and moral standards, and have been around her for a significant amount of time and you still have a hard time figuring her out, you just may be dealing with a woman that is afraid to let you fully in out of fear that you will learn who she truly is and what she is truly about.

This type of woman leads right into the worse type of person that I believe there is. That person is the liar. Never ever get involved with a person that is a compulsive liar. And believe it or not, there are millions of them. They cannot stop lying by any means. They have to lie. It is a regular part of their everyday communication. They carry all of the same ways as the sneaky ones, but they have no truth in them. In fact, some lie so much that they believe their own lies to be truths. It is unbelievable how that happens, but it does. Don't be confused or feel bad though; they lie to everyone all the same. It is not just you. Once you have dealt with one for years you will have been spun around so many times that you could possibly never believe a word that comes out of their mouth again. They lose all of your trust. They lie about small and large, life-changing issues. Once they get you on the level of never believing anything they say you can hang it up for any future in that relationship. There is very little that is worse in a relationship than a liar. It's almost like being committed to a snake. You realize that you don't even know who they truly are once it is all over. All the things that they said they wouldn't do to you, expect them to do just that now. When it comes to hurting you, or keeping you from your children, expect that they will do all that they lied and said they would never do. Everything about them, from their walk to their talk was a lie. It is a very dangerous disorder to be a liar. It is even more disastrous for you to get involved and have kids by one. The signs that a person is a compulsive liar are harder to spot at first, and take even longer to figure out how or why they are that way. Are they just like this with you, or are they like this with everyone they have dealings with? Once you get suspicious then you need to be aware. This is why I say pay attention to the right

12 Gauge Shotkids

things first. Don't get so caught up in attractions that you miss out on who the true person is. You will regret it for many years to come; and all while you are suffering all of the consequences from not carefully screening who you lay and create with.

2 LOVING AND RESPECTING THE MOTHER OF YOUR CHILD

Once you do have the right one, the next step is to learn to love and respect the mother of your child. This is a step that is unavoidable, but it is regularly disregarded. Mostly it is accidentally disregarded because most have not learned the proper ways to love and respect. This takes understanding what she is truly about and where it is that she is trying to go. It takes understanding her heart and giving up your selfish ways and feelings to accommodate hers too. This is why it is important to be a friend first before you get intimately and sexually involved, which prematurely intensifies both peoples' feelings on deeper levels. Having children with someone is more than just having a 'baby mama.' This should be your first lady. She should be the one that you are able to demonstrate the true man that you desire to be on. If every other girl that you've dealt with were 'play things' to you, this is the one that you shouldn't be playing with. Your future, and most importantly, your children's

12 Gauge Shotkids

futures all depend on how well you develop and nourish the relationship with the mother of your children. In today's society, we can notice far too many men treating the mother of their children like mere experiments. They are the ones that they damage, fuss, fight, and feud with. They are the ones that the men love to hate. But no matter what the condition of the relationship is, the mother of their children is still the one that they must interact with most. He must be concerned for her well being. They both watch each other grow.

Once you do understand her value, do yourself, her, and the kids a favor and do all that you can not to lose her trust. Don't play games with her like she is 'yours forever' no matter what. Treat her like she is as valuable as she really is. You don't want to start off a relationship with her being a liar and a cheater. If you must do these things still then you were nowhere near ready to have children with anyone. Neither man nor woman deserves to be lied to or cheated on. This displays so much immaturity and brings nothing but hell to a relationship. It seems that men get so caught up in thinking that they have a woman trapped by impregnating her that they feel it is harmless to sneak around and cheat. Constantly committing these acts and lying all of the time do nothing but break a good woman down from the inside. They turn our women cold. This is largely why we have good girls turned bad. They have been severely wounded by a careless, insensitive man that cared only for himself and not his family. The worst thing you could do in a good relationship is lose her trust. Even if you have gotten to the point where you have given up on her, this is still not the right way to go about handling your feelings. You are better off saving yourself the future regret by explaining you position, and either trying to work it out or let it go altogether. Men have a hard time letting the mother of their children go, out of fear that she will wind up with someone else, but the bitterness and anger that will be formed in her from you constantly lying and cheating will backfire on you and set off years worth of rage even after she does leave you. You are better off keeping the levels of respect higher than lower. An angry and bitter co-parent is nothing to want to deal with. Women also tend to take and build up a lot of pressure before

Soulja Soulja

they actually do explode. Spare yourself the drama because you will only later realize that it was mostly your fault to begin with. The worse feeling in the world when losing someone is to know that you hold most of the fault that they are gone. Lying and cheating on her, especially, just makes her look bad and feel even more stupid for allowing it to happen. Men have to realize that all of that built up pressure is the leading cause of the games women play against the father with the children. This is how they feel they are getting us back. And it does work. But sadly, they hurt their own children far more than they hurt the father. I believe it is the worst game ever to play, but it's being played by the best of them and it continues to be a widely popular game amongst co-parents. If we, as men, can learn at the beginning not to play our lying and cheating games we can put a huge dent in the number of female players and possibly save our children. Because the truth is, no matter who is playing what game, everyone involved gets punished in the end.

Just like being observing of her character, know that she is taking note of all that you do as well. She has her eyes on you. In fact, the more that the two of you are around one another, the more aware the two of you are towards one another's ways. She will wind up acting a lot like you, and you will have similar ways like her. This all becomes the beauty in being with someone. It's far better than being a partner with someone; the two of you become one.

While in a relationship with my children's mother, I loved this part most of all. I have a co-parent who used to be everything to me, that is younger than me by three and a half years. As I grew with her, I was able to teach her all that I knew. I was able to somewhat customize her to be who I wanted. She learned to cook what I liked to eat. We shared similar, if not the same, thoughts and life goals. Once I had put my all into her I wanted her to be a part of everything that I did. I wanted her to be about everything that I was about. This was truly the joy of having a woman. We were a team, but most importantly, we were one.

12 Gauge Shotkids

At the beginning, I did all of the things that I mentioned 'not to do' previously in this book. I played, I cheated, I lied; I didn't take the time to really get to know her before impregnating her. I also started out lacking the proper love and respect. This is how I know that these are definite 'no-no's.' I found out the hard way that kid or no kid, she will leave you. No girl or woman, no matter how gullible or air-headed that you think they are will stay around for these abuses forever. And the more quiet and air-headed you think they are you better watch out for what they plan on doing to you even more.

But I wound up getting her back sometime later, and I was sure that I was going to be the right kind of man that I've always known that I can be. I felt so much regret and hurt for what I put her through that I had to make it right. I wanted to have a healthy family and I knew that the only way to do that was to stop playing around. And I did just that.

I saw a major change in myself. I was able to become the man that I saw myself being. I couldn't raise a family healthily by running the streets and being a player. I had to become one with my partner. Not only did I have to speak this into existence, I had to show her daily. People loved to see a young, black family walk together, talk together, plan together, and smile and laugh together. What a feeling it was to get compliments on how beautiful our family was together. It was great how people were concerned when they saw one without the other. It was even better to have happy, healthy children. We both felt joy by seeing the other person's joy. If one hurt, we both hurt. What one experiences, we both experienced. Our children had a mommy and a daddy. The past was behind and the future was promising.

Becoming one with a partner is an everyday task. You grow deeper and deeper into your partner all of the time. The connection that the two of you share blocks the outside world from coming in and destroying what is being built. When love and respect has taken over, old temptations and feelings don't carry much weight anymore. You have become one with someone. You don't want,

Soulja Soulja

nor could you stand to do anything to hurt them or make them look at you differently. You want to keep them right where they're at.

This type of love and respect creates a happy home for the children. There will always be issues, but two people in tune with one another tend to get through problems much better and easier. Two out of tune people are the ones that are confused about one another and can't control bickering and fighting in front of their children. Being in a controlled environment where the parents see eye to eye also creates children who grow to be more level-headed, calm-mannered adults. All of these steps should be taken into consideration when you are the parent that is concerned about your child's future and what type of person they turn out to be. They all start watching from birth.

Equally as important is listening to your queen when she speaks. Often times being the 'macho man with the plan' tends to make us way to obsessed with what we want to do or what we say is right or wrong. You must take into consideration that the partnership consists of two people, and no one is over the other. No one person's word is greater than the other's. You can learn something by simply listening to a baby, so trust the fact that your lady has bright ideas and plans. She has opinions that are her own.

This step is a definite part of loving and respecting her. While many men suffer the wraths of their ex's rage, the majority of them still don't understand where a lot of it comes from. He is confused as to why she has given up on him or why she won't hear him out anymore. Think about how big your mouth is and how closed your mind is to her thoughts and feelings. Think about the times when you've searched for her thoughts and feelings, but really cared less or had no intention on implementing her ideas. Think about the times when she has expressed what she would like to do, or would like for you to do, and you immediately blew her off. Then you turn around and expect her to cherish every thought, idea, opinion, or plan that you have in mind. It just doesn't work like that for very long.

12 Gauge Shotkids

Women have always been very sensitive and observant humans. They are also submissive. When they have a man that is outspoken, or even self-centered, they tend to be a little more silent about expressing themselves out of fear that their expressions will be pushed off or fall on deaf ears. While some men may enjoy this act of submission, it is actually damaging to the self-esteem and confidence that a woman has. It also forces men to miss out on valuable inputs that they wouldn't or couldn't have thought up themselves, at least at the time that she presented them. It is never good, or going to produce a positive outcome for you to make your queen feel as if she has no value. If she values your ideas and thoughts you know how good that makes you feel inside and how much it motivates you to do more and communicate better. But the downfalls of devaluing her thoughts, ideas, and opinions will later on lead to her resenting yours. This is the beginning of the 'doomed relationship.' You have been so used to her hearing you out, and you not paying her any attention, that now it hurts and confuses you to see her treating you the same way. It's not that she is being mean or hating, but why should she value your innermost treasures when you treat hers as pointless? This doesn't make anyone want to support you. It actually separates the two of you. It's equivalent to being a fan of your teacher's work, then once you've learned how to do the same work or do better work, the teacher disregards your works as if they aren't good enough. That would consume you inside eventually, as you would also lose respect and start to devalue the works of your teacher now.

Men have wound up in awful situations throughout the history of life by not taking heed to their woman's feelings. They are only too busy valuing their own, but later wondering why they made the wrong turns and finding themselves feeling apologetic to her for making the mistakes that eventually hurt him, her, and the children. When it comes to dealing with a co-parent, women tend to lose just as much love and respect for you as you've shown her that you lost for her over time. The fact that her pressure pipes burst all at once makes her wrath even more dangerous, and felt even more. Again, they don't all go about things the right way, but their actions always display years of resentment and emotional

Soulja Soulja

abuse. This explains why she tries hard not to hear a word that you have to say about you, your future, or your children. She no longer wants to hear your opinion about how she is raising the children. She definitely doesn't want to hear your voice at all. It comes from so much time hearing everything 'YOU' over and over and over again. It comes from your expressionless face when she opens her mouth. Your closed mind when she is speaking her mind. It comes from your inattentiveness when she is dying to get your attention. Just imagine how she feels when she has been eager to tell you her good news all day, and when she does you indiscreetly show her how much you could care less.

Love and respect is much deeper than just saying that you love a person and respect a person. You have to show it in more ways than one. It really shouldn't be a problem to you though. Women go through great lengths for their man. They go through far greater lengths than men will go for them most times to show their love and respect for their king. It cannot be denied that someone that you claim to love and want to be with that is willing to do so much to please you makes you a proud man. We know what it's like to be alone and have no one in our corner, so to have someone that believes in us and stands by our side makes us very lucky men too. It could definitely be the other way around really fast if you make the right mistakes or say or do the wrong things, devaluing the person that you love or claim to love. And we've all had experiences with women that we didn't do our best with, and that's how we've learned about that emotional feeling known as loneliness.

The next step I want to elaborate on, which probably should've been first, is to plan to make her your wife. Never think that it is at any time a cool idea, the 'in thing to do,' or ethically or morally correct to start a family without being married, or at the very least strongly considering marriage. I put the other steps before this one because I wanted to stress the importance of getting to know a person on a friendlier level than just straight out saying 'get married.' We all know that in today's society people pop off and pop out babies without ever considering marrying the person they

12 Gauge Shotkids

are committing their life too. So it is even more important to be real when speaking on topics to today's minds.

True enough, marriage doesn't solve problems. It is not a solution. Marriage doesn't even have to mean forever, as it is intended to. But, the problem is that couples don't follow the steps that have been mentioned before either. They still lie to each other. They still cheat on each other. They are dishonest in their lifestyles. They don't try to be partners. They have just barely learned what it is to love and respect each other. All that they know is how to rush and do whatever it takes to make this 'new thang' feel however they want them to feel about them and/or the relationship they want to have with them. They fight to make their first impressions become lasting impressions. They don't think so hard about longevity. They most definitely don't think about the healthy futures of their children together.

When creating a family, make sure that is a woman that you would marry and intend on marrying. Start with getting to know everything about her. Learn how to make her your partner. Start to become one with her. Love and respect her. Marry her. People fail to realize this super valuable tip: God blesses the family that is structured right. God sees the family that is striving to be a healthy family. These couples go through hardships, but they go through them together, and it is nothing like the childish and immature problems that liars, cheaters, and deceivers go through. The ones that eliminate lies, cheats, and deceits from the equation have much more time and brain space to focus on what makes their family better and healthier. They can concentrate together on how to build. They can focus on training and bringing up their children right. They aren't worried about who the other may be with or desire to be with. They aren't worried about losing one to the streets. They don't worry about being misled by a manipulator or a lying partner. They have a higher level of respect and trust. If they argue, it's necessary arguments about a mortgage, business issues, or making the household structure better. These are arguments that the liar, cheater, and deceiver might not ever know anything about. They don't work for those blessings in their lives yet. They're still

Soulja Soulja

too focused on petty stuff. So that's what their lives will bring them.

I believe that men who have outrageous child support payments, distant and rebellious children, mothers and fathers experiencing irreconcilable differences, single parents, and problem children are all punishments for conceiving children out of wedlock and raising families the wrong way with initial ill intentions. We keep treating the mothers of our children like experimental women in our lives, but we don't even see how bad we are hurting ourselves and our futures by doing that. We initiate a slow suicide the moment that we meet these women. Since you don't know who you will marry or who will be the mother of your child you have to learn to treat all encounters with the same respect from the very start. The way that you start off the relationship, no matter how you plan to initially jump it off, that is the way that you are training yourself to be towards her throughout the relationship. Once you've started off being a certain way and giving off a certain impression it is hard to change after that. So the man that you know that you are and desire to be should show in your character from the very start. The quick mistake of being anything less than your best can be the cause of you not knowing how to advance in the relationship. You know what kind of husband you are supposed to be, but you have become stuck in pretending to be someone that you really aren't.

The mature man will treat every encounter as a possible life-long relationship. He will have experienced all that he needs to know about what kind of woman he needs and doesn't need. He will be done playing. He will be on the lookout for who could possibly become his wife. Men lose so much that they could have in their own woman, and in their lives in general, because they have never learned how important it is to get rid of their fantasies and lusts for different women. The thrill of experimenting with woman after woman consumes his mind so much that he will never find it easy to focus on the woman that is right in his face. Therefore, he doesn't learn how to bring the wife out of her, his children have parents that can't come together fully, he doesn't learn to become the man he is supposed to be, he never has anyone that truly loves and cares about him, and he never experiences a fulfilling life. There's even married men that still lust and fantasize over different women, then wonder why their marriage is slowly crumbling even without getting caught up. They look for every excuse except their own dangerous minds. This is why you have to become one with your queen. Outsiders throw you off of your square and cause you to lose focus on the one you need to keep focus on. Men fail to realize that they can get their woman to be all that they are seeking from other women. But to men, it is more thrilling to chase separate personalities and pleasures. And when you seek, you shall find. And once you do, you can count on the home that you built being taken apart brick by brick. Don't think that just because you can sneak and get away with it for months or years that you aren't slipping and making your woman feel like you are doing her wrong. There are more ways to get caught slipping than there are cover-ups. Your behavior and attitude will be the dead giveaway.

But when you are on the right track in the relationship, understand that people grow and people change. You and her will have different needs at times. Make sure that you are paying attention to her changes and make changes with the flow of the relationship. I always tell people to stop being so comfortable after being with their mate for some time. Never cease at making them see a new you. Never cease at recreating them in ways that suit both of you. Some people do the same things over and over. They wear the same clothes over and over. They don't even think to make their other half more appealing to them. Also, women tend to want to move ahead faster. They may take more interest in buying instead of renting. They may start wanting to take trips. They may want you to give up old, unhealthy habits for obvious reasons. You have to make these changes, and not be so quick to disregard them. This leads to an unhealthy relationship. Just like you see different women at different stages of appeal and progression, your woman sees men the same way. She wants you to stand out as well. She will get tired of you being the same looking and doing the same stuff. Paying attention to her changing mind and her new growth will teach you how to keep her heart and her mind on you, and only you. Don't expect her to just be the same as she was when

Soulja Soulja

you met her, especially if she was under twenty-five years old when you met her. These young ladies grow into women that start to want more and more out of life. Only a foolish man will lounge around the house all day sleeping, dressing poorly, having no ambitions, and not daring to do different. Women love new things and new adventures. But do not forget that while you are recreating yourself, remember her. Buy her new things and make her feel special too. You will keep your household in compliance that way.

3 WHEN THE RELATIONSHIP CAN'T WORK

As long as you've tried your hardest and done all that you can do, it is still a chance that it may not work out. It's ok though when the relationship can be severed with no hard feelings. Sometime two people grow out of one another. Sometime the differences and disagreements make it impossible to keep up with the same person and lifestyle. Women can change faster than men a lot of times. While men can keep up at the same pace, tolerating the usual, women will be faster to just give it up. When the woman wants to go, you have to let her go. No matter how much you love her or don't want to see her with anyone, you have to let her go. This is much easier thought up and said than it actually is to do, but it is very important and true. As much as it takes a person that truly loves you and been through much with you to give up, once they do, it is rare that their feelings can be overturned. If you are the reason that she changed up, then you definitely will have little chance at driving her back in love with you.

Soulja Soulja

It becomes very unsettling when there are children involved. The thought of either your children growing up without you in the household or growing up with another man around is painful. Even still, it is much better to let her go than to develop a toxic relationship that is consistently brewing anger, bitterness, and growing hatred. This will be much more harmful to the children than another man being around them.

Sometime a woman just need to go for reasons unknown that don't really have much to do with you, but her intentions are to at least try and save your heart and your friendship in the long run. It is often harder for a person, male or female, to say to their partner that they want to experience a life with someone else or to explain to them how the other isn't keeping up with the lifestyle that they see themselves living and pursuing. Some women haven't learned their own independence levels yet. They want to experience being single for a while. Maybe you aren't who they initially thought you were in the beginning. There are a host of reasons that women and men decide to end a relationship. As long as you know that she has always displayed responsibility and carefulness, don't expect her to all of a suddenly become reckless. If she has always portrayed a good parent with great parenting skills, don't expect her to all of a suddenly be any less than that. Men can conjure numerous false accusations and negative feelings once they have lost control and/or touch with their woman. These feelings and accusations are purely fictional and based on fear of our doubt, our frustrations, and overall our loss. Keep positive thoughts unless you see otherwise with your eyes, not your mind. The mind is extremely misleading during times like these, considering all of the life changes that are presently occurring. The mind will cause you to do very ignorant, out of character things, and say very disrespectful and untruthful words. The part about her finding someone else could be a fear that he may be somewhat better for her right now than you. This is almost always wrong. I hate to say it with a smile on my face, but women tend to get someone else who is either not very much different, or even worse than her ex. If her choosing skills were that good that she could just easily go out and do so much better she wouldn't have had you in the first place. If she

12 Gauge Shotkids

was attracted to you then she is attracted to people similar to you. By her getting someone else, that should be motivation for you to step it up a few notches on him and her. You can play the background and dish out some heavy competition then. It is never as bad as your mind will make it seem though. Let her go and let her figure out along the way what she has lost.

You never have to worry about someone taking over your children when you are already a great father. This just can't happen. Children always know who their dad is no matter if their mom has twenty men. As long as you stay active, don't let your mind make you think otherwise. Nor should a good mother ever make her children choose between her boyfriend and their father. Immature, irresponsible, and petty behaviors in a woman should be checked and considered at the time you meet and get to know them to prevent having kids by the type that will possibly let another man take over her and your children's lives. This does happen too.

If you were to pay attention to her earlier along, maybe even just before she breaks it off with you, you may be able to see what it is that is making her change on you. Maybe if you were to listen to her complaints and concerns you could hear what is bothering her. Every woman gives off these signals and vibes before she breaks it off for good. She may even have threatened to leave you several times before, but didn't. These words and actions come back to bite you when they are taken lightly. Don't be silly and naïve about the situation; no happy person will leave or threaten to leave you. For your sake and your children's sake, you need to examine what it is that she is feeling. You may be able to make some drastic changes and prevent the break-up altogether.

All a woman wants to be is loved, respected, and happy. At any point when she is lacking one of these she will become skeptical about your place in her life. The best thing that you can do, and that she is dying for you to do, is to change that. She wants you to acknowledge what you are doing wrong and not just speak about it, but be about taking the steps to restore her faith in you. It is when we overlook the problem and say that we don't care, and act like

Soulja Soulja

we don't care, that causes us to lose good women. We can really let our ego and pride get the best of us and destroy everything that we have built. You won't believe how easy it is to regain control over our household and our relationship by getting rid of selfishness, stubbornness, and being egotistical jerks. These women will not stay with us forever being unhappy. It is so much better to nip the problem before she is completely fed up. It is nearly impossible to fully restore them back once you've allowed them to go so far into disappointment. Everything you do from that point on won't mean a thing. This even goes for the voiceless woman that you are so used to that does everything you tell her to do and says nothing behind it. If you find yourself not giving concern to, or not caring about her feelings or thoughts, you can count on losing her soon.

All it really takes is observing, having compassion, and making the necessary changes, and then you can save your relationship from disaster. Do all of these things before she can ever mention there is a problem if you pick up on it fast enough. A woman that isn't quite done with you, and still has a grain of faith in you, will draw herself back into your world. As long as you are serious and consistent she will react as if she never felt any indifference. If you think that it is a high priority and it's mandatory that your children grow with their mother and father in a healthy relationship and household, imagine how she feels about that. Imagine how much more she wants that to be a reality. She will do anything in her power to see to it that she stays on the right track and doesn't do anything to jeopardize that reality. Even if it means that she has to take the good with the bad when it comes to you. A woman will absorb all kinds of pains in hopes that you will eventually listen and recognize, and ultimately learn the right way to treat her and build the family. This is why it makes total sense to do what you need to do to satisfy her. The sacrifices that she makes for you have a great impact on the relationship, but often go unseen.

Spare yourself from the discomfort and anguish from knowing that you lost her when you could have made some simple changes. Think about how important it is to have your family together. This

12 Gauge Shotkids

pain from discomfort creates that unstable mindset and the bitterness that you feel once she moves on. It's too late to plead and beg. You should have tried to do that before she left. All of the signs pointed right to how she was feeling and what you needed to do to change that. If she still decides to leave the relationship on down the road, the changes you made were still for the better. You don't want to have to face her and your children throughout life knowing that you did wrong, but did nothing to make it right. This doesn't always keep them forever, but at least you have a clear conscience and you free yourself to allow yourself to move on easier without feeling like you need to have her back just to prove to her that you can do her right. For the most part, at least you will go into your next relationship a better partner that was taught a valuable lesson.

But hey, just because she leaves doesn't mean that she will stay gone. Believe it or not, they usually return. If you can get past your mind playing tricks, and all of the negative feelings and just let her go, you may be able to see she didn't quite go too far. As long as you play the background and not stress her every move and every whereabouts, giving her the upper hand and allowing her to play on your emotions, you may just get your family right back.

Most times we have been such a dominant force in our woman's life that she feels like she needs time to find herself and breathe. And our problem is we feel like she can't do that. There is nothing wrong with her doing this. Men often feel like they need the same thing when they have been smothered by the same person for so long. Sadly, some men will just start spending more time away from home and occasionally in other women's beds before they talk to their other half about time to breathe. A woman may choose to split up for a while to avoid lying, sneaking, and cheating. This is a very good thing. Most times our black women have had a child and a co-parent before they've even moved out of their parent's home. They may have never had as many encounters with men as they've desired to experience. By encounter, I mean finding out other personalities and characters that may align with the lifestyle she wants. All of these things are important for her to experience

Soulja Soulja

so that she can feel fulfilled later on in life and be able to understand what it is that she really wants and doesn't want. She'll learn what she needs and doesn't need. She'll probably learn that she was just fine with you.

Our children's mothers have children at such a young age that there is no way for them to understand who they truly are or what they can do, especially when they have a man that they must be committed to, and without the kid or kids, they probably would have been went in another direction a long time ago. This is bound to create confusion in her by the time she starts hitting the ages between twenty one and thirty. She must move around, which will eventually be a part of her growth. Just give her time to see what she feels she needs to see, and if and when she does come back or not, she should be a much better and advanced person that understands herself more.

Just like men, we think that the grass is greener elsewhere. We think that the first impression of another woman will last forever. We are attracted to what we see and think that is what we want. We either give up on what we have or secretly go out and experience it while still trying to keep what we already have. Nine times out of ten we experience it enough to realize that it is not what we want. We learn that the one that we have is the one that we need. We discover how important our family being together is. Women and men experience the same feelings, which create the doubts in our relationships. But this type of thinking usually means that we aren't completely focused on and committed to who we have in the first place. This is slightly different than needing to find yourself. It's sort of like a hidden agenda. It does tend to happen to people though. When it does happen, and the desire is fulfilled, the drifter finds themselves drifting right back to the one that loved them in the beginning. That's why we can't go chasing fantasies. You will happen to have given up your family for someone that doesn't even love you or never will learn to love you right. They may even be selling dreams with no intention of ever making good on their commitments. You have to be leery about people who are willing to break up your family when they know

12 Gauge Shotkids

you have one. You don't need to worry so much when your woman thinks she found something better. When she spent all of her time being committed to you, how do you think she had time to properly screen who she thinks is so called' better than you?' You can believe that there are the highest chances of that situation crumbling like a cookie before it can even really get started. They can force a miserable relationship if they want, but two people who barely know one another can't last together for long without getting to know one another first, and that takes years. As long as you remain level-headed and calm throughout the whole ordeal, expect her to recognize what she has gotten herself into and what she has lost, and she may come crawling back.

With all of that being said, you will run into a problem with her resenting you and later on hating you when you call yourself forcing her to stay. When you start letting all of the negative feelings and thoughts get the best of you, this usually becomes the outcome. Also, the emotional rollercoaster of guilt will make you react the wrong way when dealing with a break-up. But doing whatever it is that you are doing to make her stay will actually backfire on you in the end. The resistance that she gives you can cause serious frustration and confusion, which can lead to verbal, emotional, and sometimes physical abuse.

As I've stated before, it is very hard to bring a woman back to the way you've known her once she is already gone. You have to let her see what she feels she needs to see. She needs to become who God is shaping her to become without you getting in the way of that plan. Forcing her to stay with you only makes you feel like a fool later on. Sometimes the words you say and the nice things that you do may stimulate temporary feelings in her that are satisfactory to you, and may cause you to think you've won her back, but trust that she will snap right back into her new reality of what it is that she really wants to do. You only give her the opportunity to play on your feelings when you display weakness. Just because your life may feel like it is over, and your heart is torn, that doesn't mean that she does or is trying to feel your pain. The old saying 'when someone wants to leave just let 'em go'

Soulja Soulja

means so much because it keeps you from saying things, good or bad, that don't need to be said. I recall feeling like I was going to win my girl back at one point by confessing all of my wrongdoings that I committed on her. I also explained how much I regretted those things and how serious I was about changing them. Boy did that backfire on me. All I did was confess so much that she didn't know, and didn't need to know, that I didn't realize how I just told her how much I was a lying, sneaking, cheating, deceiver. I revealed to her how often I disrespected her and had no regards for the way she felt while I was doing what I was doing. This made her feel even better about her decision to leave me. So while I thought I was doing her a favor and drawing her back to me, I was really pushing her further away. You have to be careful about what you say. It's better to say nothing at all, although that is easier said than done. If there is something you need to apologize about, do that and move on. When it is in an attempt to get her back, the opposite will happen. She has no desire to be with you, and it shows, because God is transitioning her. She probably doesn't even understand fully why she feels how she feels. All she knows is that she can't help it. And that is all because God has put her in the passenger seat now. You are no longer the driver either.

Forcing her to stay will only stop her from growing mentally and will keep the two of you at one another's throats. You then open yourself up to be played and preyed on. It's something about when a woman can hear your heart crying out, seeing your tears from hurt and regret, and feels you tugging at her every second of the day; she loves that. She will continue to drag you through the mud for as long as she can. In some cases, men have been so lost and confused and hurt by this and that and they have literally snapped out and injured or killed the mother of their children. The negative feelings and thoughts led them to burglarize, stalk, physically abuse, vandalize, and all sorts of criminal acts. Instead of letting her go, they pushed themselves to their limits, without even caring about themselves or their children. No woman on earth is worthy enough to snap out over and wind up behind bars for even a day and a case. But it will happen if you lose it over them. When you wind up behind bars, she is still going to do what she was going to

12 Gauge Shotkids

do, regardless. Don't be a fool by going through all kinds of extents to make them stay. The kids are the silent sufferers when mom wants to go but can't. They have to listen to the endless arguments and deal with an unhappy mother and a hurt father. They get caught up in the middle of the love/hate war. Two parents that are only worried about how they feel will very easily overlook the watchful eyes and listening ears of a child. You can only make matters worse for all parties involved by forcing her to stay. Like it was mentioned before, the sooner you back off, the less you will make a mistake you will live to regret. If she wants to go, she will do just that. All of the feelings that you and her have, all of the anger, and the separation is all because neither of you are in control anymore. And normally for people, we have a difficult time dealing with change. And this is a big change for us, but it has to be done and will be done. But it will all be done for the better in the end. We just can't see that now, it doesn't make a lick of sense to us, so we naturally take it hard and try to stay in control of a situation that is already dead.

4 LOVING YOUR CHILDREN MORE THAN YOU HATE THEIR MOTHER

What is interesting is how a man that is hurt and deep down wants the mother of his children back will do the exact opposite of what he should be doing to get her back. His heart tells him to let her go, but his mind says pursue her even more and harder. His heart says that he loves her, but his mind says hurt her in every way possible. His heart says to be nice, courteous, and gentle when handling her and communicating with her, but his mind says cuss her out. The worst of them all is when his heart says it's all about the kids from now on, but his mind says 'I'll get back at her by not doing for the kids.' This is where the games have gone too far.

Thou shall never, ever, ever stop doing for his children in order to keep up the games with their mother. This is a commandment. I personally stand on this, and a man could never get any love or respect from me as a father for continuing to violate this. It

12 Gauge Shotkids

happens so often though. A man that has been there for his kids all of their lives will have the audacity to think that this will maybe bring her back, or hurt her deeper. Newsflash, you can't hurt a woman by not being there for YOUR kids. She will only recognize you as the petty, deadbeat, weak daddy that you are becoming. The one you hurt is the children. Not doing for your kids won't make her run back to you or keep the next man that you are so worried about out of her house. If she comes back to you for pulling this beyond stupid stunt she is just as much as a fool as you are becoming. It kills me how many men do the exact opposite of what it actually takes to not only get a woman back, although in many cases he doesn't even want her back, but to remain appealing and respectable to her after the split. This is what makes her think twice about what decisions she made. How does becoming any less of a father supposed to make her think that she made the wrong decision by flipping you? The lifetime commitment that you have with this particular woman should make her one of the main women that you want to see you at your best at all times. You never want her to see you being weak; you never want her to see you being deadbeat. This goes beyond wanting her back.

A father should always do for his children no matter what the situation is with their mother. The more you can't get along with the mother, the better you should get along with the children. See, when you find yourself concerned about what the mother may be up to, although you can't stop it, you can always pull your children away from it. You may worry about another man playing 'daddy' to them, but how could he do that when you have them just as much as she does, if not more? Where we as fathers get ourselves messed up at from the start is playing games that start the mother's counterattacks. We say harsh things that ignite her and cause her to be vengeful and spiteful. Although none of it is good, and all of it is petty and childish, it's our reality. We have to continue to concentrate on doing. We have to concentrate on doing more for our children. If you can eliminate the name calling, poking, and ill will and focus on the mother from the start you will experience far less and maybe even no game playing at all. When you want to play, play with your child.

Soulja Soulja

I know these things to be true because I used to have my child with me but could still be so focused on her mother and what she is doing or who she's with that I didn't even notice my own child sitting right next to me. My visit with my child would come and go like my baby was never even really there. That is not cool at all, and I learned to change that over the years. These kids deserve attentive and focused adults as parents. I never could stop doing for mine, but I definitely have neglected their need for attention at times because I was so concerned about their mother at times when I shouldn't have been. The best thing that I learned to do was to let her see how much of a dedicated and proud parent that I was. The only way she could see that was when she had no choice but to notice how 'not worried' I was about her.

I stress the importance of being able to let go and focusing only on your children when the relationship doesn't work because there is a high number of men sitting behind bars because of the emotions they have to deal with when they can't let go of these women. All of the cases don't surround a child's mother, but the mother of a person's children is the number one victims in these cases.

We have to face it. Men play hard, but most are very tender. They are especially tender over women. They get even softer to the touch when that woman is their co-parent. In fact, when you hear about beef in the streets or a man getting killed by another man he didn't even know, nine times out of ten the drama stemmed from a woman. A man can't stand for another man to be involved with his 'baby mama.' This causes one on one drama, all the way down to gang/clique violence. One man gets into it over a woman and all of a suddenly a set of crews and cliques don't like each other and don't even know where the problem originated. There is all of this chaos because men don't know how to let go. They worry about all of the wrong things in which they have no control over.

I have had harsh words thrown back and forth over the mother of my kids before I knew better, but never any violence that stemmed from it. What I have been guilty of is having thoughts about harming the mother of my kids. All of this was before I knew

12 Gauge Shotkids

better. I have even heard other fathers rant about what they would do to their co-parent if she ever did some of the things that I explained to them that mine has done to me, or what they have already done to theirs to get them in compliance. I have heard about some gunning the mother down and others that beat them down. They rob and steal from them. They pay people to do harm to them. There are even some that will kidnap and rape them.

When I heard this, I immediately changed the way I felt toward my co-parent. I was resentful that I even entertained the thoughts. Just as sure as I would hope that she doesn't wish any harm on me, I don't want to wish it on her. Now I can't believe or grasp how an ignorant man could want to see his co-parent dead, hurt, or suffering. In most cases, this was the woman that you once loved and cared for. She gave birth to the best creations that you will ever make. She raises them the best that she can. Most of all, they love her just like you love your mother. If you couldn't imagine someone taking your mother from you, how could you dare entertain the thought of taking yours from theirs? You have to be the devil himself. There is no way you are a child of God. The day that it becomes cool to kill or hurt the mother of your children will be the day it will be cool for her to take them out of your life permanently for any reason. Just because she gets under your skin, it by no means justifies you hurting her in any kind of way, for any reason. We have to realize that some things we can't control and we just have to let God deal with it, and He most certainly will. If you take matters into your own hands, you take all of the blame for the outcome. If you kill or hurt her you go to jail and the kids have no mother or father now. What kind of parent wants that for his/her kids? Was what you felt really that deep that it became the only solution? A dead mother and an incarcerated father is no good life for children. And to think, it was all because daddy was mad about another man that most likely was not even going to be a lasting threat, if any at all. We must trust that God will make it right. It's usually the man that lacks the faith and turns vengeful and violent. He sees no way but his way. But to the man that thinks of harming or killing one of God's children, you can believe that if God isn't ready for her to go yet He will find a way to get rid of you to

Soulja Soulja

prevent you from disturbing her and His plan for her. Think about how often you seem to get caught up. It might be time to change the plotting and negative feelings and thoughts. Chances are you may be only killing and hurting yourself.

Another way to kill yourself and to ruin a positive future with your co-parent and the kids is to use the children as weapons. This is another way that men can use a game that they think they will win and they will do the exact opposite. Using kids as weapons is just like using a regular firearm on a person. It is a game that is very harmful to all parties, especially the children.

Using children as weapons means that one or both parents are engaged in using the children to hurt the other. They can try to do this a number of ways. The most common way is to not let the other parent have any visitation or little to no communication with the children. Another way is to reveal things to the child to get them to dislike, or even hate the other parent. A parent may even go as far as to coerce a child to do harmful things to the other parent or their property while the child is with that parent. A parent will use a child as a weapon when they have no other strategy to get back at a co-parent that they know is in love with their child. This is the only way that they can find that will hurt them. It is very true; a child is the best weapon against a loving parent. When a parent is denied visitation or contact with their child, it can send their life spiraling out of control. It will also cause them to want to hurt somebody, and in turn, put them at risk of getting into trouble. All of these outcomes sound just fine to the parent that is sending the attacks. But what's not recognized at first is that all of that evil comes right back to them.

The best thing to do when you are under attack is to do exactly what you are supposed to be doing as a parent and back off of every other level. Don't feed into self-fueled arguments, don't pick fights, and don't show any signs of weakness. When women that will do these things to you keep attacking it will hurt like hell but smile in her face. Do not let her see or think for one second that she is getting the best of you. You have to remain bigger than her

12 Gauge Shotkids

and her games. If you are denied your visitation, don't act a fool. There are steps that you will have to take to get that in order. A mother that continues to pick at you can't win a game that you aren't bothering to play with her. She can only make herself look and feel bad.

A man that uses his kids as a weapon against their mother will suffer very similar defeats. Children will grow up to understand that their father did evil things to their mother, and he will pay for those things. God doesn't like to see adults causing harm to children, and turning kids against a parent is emotionally abusive to a child. The whole thought process behind it is selfish and immature. There is no way that any parent can justify hurting a parent with children. Who do they think they are hurting more, the grown-up or the helpless child? Any real parent wouldn't think for a second of doing anything that would hurt their child. But that is the first problem; they don't see what they're doing as an issue so they don't think about what effect their actions will have on the child. They only care about satisfying their own pain, hurt, and anguish. I despise parents like this. They run and confess to the world how much they love and do for their children, but secretly they do everything in their power to turn the child against the other parent. Even those that threaten the co-parent with alienating them from their family are bad parents in my eyes. They have no concern for the emotional strain that puts on their babies.

Using children as weapons is a quick way to put a halt to blessings for your near future. People who play games wonder why they keep on winning their own games but never get the chance to see a prize. The smart victim won't let you beat them when they can recognize that you are playing a dangerous game. Parents can easily draw bad luck onto them and not even know it. In fact, while they are so busy playing, how can they see that? They take matters into their own hands and don't even realize that God has something in store for them. People also lose their lives by playing with folks' children. You can't expect for everyone to be calm and well mannered when they love and miss their children. Me personally, I know how much I love both of my parents and I

Soulja Soulja

would never want to deny my own children the right to do the same with theirs. In that case, my thoughts and feelings for their mother don't matter.

When you are going through these difficult times, no matter how good or bad the situation is, always keep the children in mind. Ultimately, if it weren't for the children being there the split wouldn't be so difficult anyways. It's just way too many emotions being thrown around surrounding the well being of the kids, on top of losing a partner, that kids often are the last ones who's feelings are considered when it comes down to getting your point across or making your wrath felt. Parents that aren't paying attention to their children more than they are paying attention to the words and actions of one another will very easily be the ones that put their children right in the middle of the war.

In order for a child to have a pleasant childhood during a split-up between two parents that they deserve to have together doing the right things, they have to be totally excluded from the adult business and drama. Far too many inconsiderate mothers and fathers completely miss this part while satisfying their own agendas with the other parent. They don't even think before they impulsively jump on the phone and blatantly bash the other parent right in front of the children. They jump on the phone, and in the presence of their friends, they do the same thing. They speak horribly about the other parent in front of kids that love that parent unconditionally. These same people will fight and kill someone for talking about a friend of theirs in this manner. Yet, they feel it is alright to speak in this way about someone's parent right in front of them. Some even do this on purpose so that the child can hear and know stuff they have no business knowing. They elaborate on adult issues in front of them and to them.

Children are meant to stay in children's places. They have no business absorbing with their premature minds what adults know or feel about another parent, unless it is all good things. Kids are not put here for anything except to eat, sleep, play, learn, love, and grow. Anything being displayed to, said, or done to a child that is

12 Gauge Shotkids

intended to make them dislike, hate, or mislead another is absolutely wrong and despicable. One thing about a child that loves their parent is that it is going to be extremely hard for the other parent to change that. Unless that parent is hurting or damaging the child they will greatly resent anyone, including a parent, who is set out on degrading the other parent. Even if a parent is hurting a child, you have to do what you can to comfort them outside of talking bad about them. Children grow to understand who has hurt them on their own and they act accordingly with that person. It is not your job as a parent to sway their feelings. It won't make the child love you any more than they already do. Their minds are simply too young to comprehend what they need to do. But if you try making them feel indifferent about a parent, you make them feel like it is some way that they are supposed to feel, or that it is something that they are supposed to do about it. This is how kids are rushed into being grown. A parent may have put too much on their mind at an early age.

All of this is not only just about bashing a parent to a child. It also involves other things that parents encounter when they end up taking on the kids alone after a split. Some parents complain about utility and food consumption. Kids grow rapidly; they eat more and use more utilities. This is all a part of raising children. Don't blame them and fuss at them. You can train them to turn off lights and water or teach them about not wasting so much food, but never make them feel bad, because they can pick up on your vibe and feel your pain. It pains them not to be able to help. They should never be worried about the bills or your dealings with other adults and adult situations. Only talk to them like children, and about children's situations. Kids can take adult business in the wrong ways and even spread it to others all wrong. You will never know what they lay their little heads on their pillow and think about what they've taken in. There are way too many grownups that have very little memory of, or have totally blocked out their childhoods, because of words and situations that were put into their heads. Most were rushed to grow fast and didn't have much of a childhood. You should want for your children to have much of a childhood, with steady growth, but no rush to be grown. The ones that get to be thirteen to seventeen years old and always hollering about 'I can't wait to be grown' are usually the ones that had parents that rushed them by involving them in adult business while they were much too young. Believe me when I tell you that a parent has a hard time knowing they are doing this if they aren't paying attention to themselves. They think it is alright to sit up giggling, laughing, and cursing and discussing everything under the sun in front of their kids, not even seeing how much of it the kids are absorbing. It all backfires on them later though. It's only cool to drink, smoke, and curse in front of your kids until the kids become teenagers and start costing you money and causing you problems for drinking, drugging, and filthy behaviors and attitudes. One thing that is for sure is that the kids are always intrigued and paying attention to everything, especially negativity. The more you make it look and sound good, the more they can't wait to mimic it.

What is really good is when you are going through these times and you dedicate your time to your children by becoming more active and involved in what they are doing or could be doing. This usually never happens at the beginning of the split, but should definitely be picked up before you lose yourself to anger and bitterness. See, we don't get to put the entire family back together sometime, so you have to enhance and build on what you do have, and the kids aren't going anywhere. The best part about becoming more involved is that you get to discover things about your parental abilities that you didn't even know existed. As fathers, we are used to letting the mother handle most of the workload. We pick and choose what it is that we want to do. We usually do the manly things with the kids. When you have the kids now, you have to learn to do everything. You learn to listen more, play more, teach more, and you even find yourself cooking and cleaning more. All of these things are good because getting so involved with the children makes you much less worried about their mother and what she is doing.

The kids respect an active father so much and the rewards are great. There is nothing like seeing happy children. No child wants to see an unhappy, lost father that can't seem to find energy and

12 Gauge Shotkids

drive to pick himself up. They want a father that takes them out to fun places; they want a father that cares about what they talk about. They love to see dad pop up at school. Being an active, involved parent when it comes to the child's academics is probably the most important and valuable things you can do. It never hurts to take time out and pick your child's brain and see what type of things interest them, seriously. They often talk so much that you can't quite figure out what they would be serious about. They grow so rapidly in the mind and body that you have to periodically take time out to see where they're at. Once you find these things out, see what you can possibly do to stimulate their skills. Getting them involved in extracurricular activities gives them and you something more to do besides sitting around the house. Above all, you want to make sure you are doing all that you can to promote a positive, healthy kid that is loving life and learning.

Children are much more interested in sharing their thoughts and ideas with a parent that they know is interested. Most importantly, they are quicker to share their concerns with you and you definitely need that. You need to know who or what is bothering them at all times, if any. It is harder for someone to brainwash them into not going to an active, involved parent that they know cares and will react immediately to whatever. Kids want to do more with their lives when they aren't so afraid of mommy and daddy saying no or being discouraging. When you find something out that they are very interested in, do your best to make it happen. Don't be so quick to brush them off and say no. This will easily make them not want to do anything with themselves.

5 ESTABLISHING PATERNITY AND VISITATION

An important part of being an unmarried father that is greatly overlooked is establishing paternity for your children. Men seem to think that just because they sign a birth certificate or that they have raised a child since birth that it makes them the father. Although that does make you the father in your eyes and everyone else's eyes, it means very little to the court system. You can get around establishing paternity as long as you and the mother are in an active relationship. But as soon as you and her split, you should be prepared for all hell to break loose.

It is not as simple as a mother telling you that she won't do this and that to you if the two of you were to split. When a relationship is going good, she will always have your best interest in mind. They all say that they won't keep your kids from you, ever. They will despise others that do that to their co-parent. She will always say that she won't put you on child support as long as you are

12 Gauge Shotkids

actively taking care of the child. She will always say that she won't deny you your parental rights. But it never fails that as soon as the relationship ends, and especially if it has a bitter ending, she goes and does everything that she said she wouldn't do. A very small percentage of women that have bitter breakups actually hold on strong to their initial words. The rest of them, you are in big trouble if you don't get paternity established. I don't know if it is a hot topic amongst mothers, but they all seem to know that a father that hasn't been to court at all for his children have no say so in any matter relating to the children until they actually do go to court. This is where they know they can get a weak father every time, and they can control how he interacts with his children.

So, the smart father knowing all of this would get paternity established as soon as possible. The problem that the father faces when it comes to going in front of the court system to establish paternity is that they wind up putting themselves on child support. But if the smart father were to think ahead, he would handle the paternity situation while he and the mother were still on good terms. This way he could possibly avoid paying child support to her while they are together and raising the child together. Although, it may be different in some places, a mother can opt to not have a father pay child support or stop child support payments. All of this is unless the mother is receiving cash assistance from the state, and then the father is left no choice but to reimburse the state. If the father handled it this way he wouldn't have to worry about going through a lengthy court process during the heat of a breakup just to establish that he is the father of the kids. This gives the mother lots of time and room to play whatever games that she wants with him and the children while the father has to wait one to six months just to get into court.

Establishing paternity simply involves stating to the court that you are the father of said child/children if you've signed birth certificates, or taking a DNA test on said child or children if you claim to be the father but didn't sign a birth certificate. It is fairly easy, with no headache involved. The procedures may also vary from state to state. The courts will then set up visitation and child support. As long as both parties are level-headed adults the courts will let the parents make all the arrangements and schedules. Establishing paternity gives the father an equal amount of rights to the child as the mother though. It makes sense to the have to have paternity established as there would be a huge number of children that are being claimed by the wrong fathers if not. For many years, women have blamed babies on men who aren't really the father, and men have claimed babies without actually knowing if they are really the father. Establishing paternity makes it clear that you can take a DNA test and know for sure, or just off of signing the birth certificate you can accept responsibility. It is a medium that will bring deceitful situations to light if there was some untruthfulness on the mother's part when the baby was conceived. Besides the father gaining parental rights, he never has to worry much about a mother who later denies him as the father and tries to control everything involving the child.

They will do just that when they know that you don't have rights. A bitter mother will do all that she can to turn you away from your kids in order to hurt you. Where most fathers go wrong is they don't take action through the courts. They either don't know how, are afraid to, or want to just avoid going to court altogether. The father doesn't understand the process a lot of the time because the men around him don't understand either. Most men know that the majority of the men they are around are not active fathers. They rarely discuss their children and they definitely don't give good advice on what to do to handle establishing their rights. This leads to a high number of men who simply give in and give up to the pressures of a mother who already has the upper hand to begin with.

Just because a mother has the upper hand doesn't mean that the father's hands are broken though. The father simply has to learn what his rights are when dealing with the mother, and the courts. I can't explain enough how valuable it is to learn all that you can while dealing with your rights as a father. Not only do you have rights as a father, the child also has rights. These rights are enforceable as long as you know what you are doing and what you

12 Gauge Shotkids

are fighting for. Just knowing that you have rights is enough to give you hope that you can prevail. This hope is what will ensure that you never give up. The problem with giving up is that there is no one else to fight for the children and their rights. A child definitely can't fight. Some mothers make it so hard for a father in so many ways and it can prove to be the most difficult time of a man's life. It is sad to say and see a man have to fight to see his own children, but a great deal of mothers sadly makes this a reality. It is sad to see a great deal of mothers make false claims and accusations with the intent of damaging the credibility and reputation of a father, or getting him incarcerated on bogus charges, but it is our world nowadays.

You have to learn your rights and your child's rights. You can't let either them or yourself suffer at the hands or tongue of a mother that will eventually live to regret her actions once the smoke clears. Another very important decision you have to make while going at this battle is that you will always prevail as long as you have the child's best interest in mind. This is all that matters to the courts, and it should be all that matters to you. Often times, you have a father that knows his rights but he tries to go at the mother's neck just as hard as she is going at his. Now you have both parents going as hard as they can to take over the kids and damage the other parent. Neither even tries to realize what is in the best interest of the child. This is where you will lose yourself and steer totally in the wrong direction as the father.

In an attempt to gain control, you may find a parent who tries to take over custody of the child, knowing the task is too much for them to handle for various reasons. Either parent can be the parent that is not suitable enough to provide the child a better life. It varies from family to family. Smart parents will put the child with the parent that they are better off with. It shouldn't ever be confused with just because 'you are the mother' the kids automatically belong with you. They may be better off with a more 'well-off' father. It's all about who can provide for them better. This is even if it is for just some time. Smart parents consider and negotiate this intelligently. A parent that doesn't have the best interest of the child but fights for their own self-fulfilling, egotistical reasons will be the loser in the end. They will eventually lose control, despite what a court has to say. Life will have a way at snapping them into reality. So when you are a parent that has the child's best interest in mind don't worry too hard about a co-parent's temporary victories. They won't last long before the games start to catch up to them.

Learn your rights so that you can better control the situation and control yourself at the same time. You will have a much higher chance of not wanting to give up if you know that your attempts will pay off because you have your child's best interest in mind. It is also much easier to deal with the court system when you have an idea of what to expect, and what you're talking about. There are books that you can check out at your local library or you can talk to other parents that have been in similar situations, but you have to remember that every case is different and you need to know the specifics to every law and all of the rights that pertain to your unique case. Searching the internet is very useful too. You need to learn all of the different petitions to file, and how and where to file. The only way to be taken seriously is to actually know. Some fathers don't even know that grandparents have rights too. So if something were to happen to you, your parents don't have to lose out on being in the kids' lives. There are numerous amounts of literature available that will successfully get you through to the next step when dealing with a mother that wants to go to war. The faster you learn it, the faster you get on top of it and beat her at her own game. All that the woman usually knows is how to keep custody of the kids. That's easy for her. She doesn't even know about the rights that you and the children have. Just refrain from letting your left hand know what the right hand is doing, and you could very well achieve satisfactory results in the fight for rights.

The child support issue is one that fathers go through great lengths to avoid. A lot of children go without fathers nowadays all because of fear of paying child support. A lot of fathers still go without seeing their children even though they pay child support. Some fathers don't pay child support and want to be active in the

12 Gauge Shotkids

children's lives, but are still denied time with the children by the mother because they aren't getting paid. Child support is a huge issue that I believe needs a lot of reform, but should not be looked at as anything but a good situation for the children. It is often misused, which makes it such a dramatic topic.

Child support is meant to be exactly as the name says. It is support for your child. Fathers should not look down on child support or fear it. When child support is used correctly it feeds, shelters, clothes, and provides for our children. There should be nothing wrong with that, and it should be embraced. It is a steady payment that contributes our portion in providing for our kids. Most of us, when dealing with absence, distance, and/or a bitter relationship ending, will find it harder to just fork over money to provide for our children. Not only that, how will you know how much is enough? How many of us would participate or do it consistently? A system had to be put in place that would make it easier to care for the family. The keywords mentioned were 'care for the family.' One thing about it is that when you, the father, created that family you vowed to care for that family forever. When a man backs out of this commitment this is why he looks stupid and gets called the names he does for showing his irresponsibility and weakness. You made the family; you take care of that family. Kids and creating families were never said to be anything to play with. Everyone knows that it is hard work and a lifelong process so it should be treated as such, even if you have problems with the co-creator or not. Child support should not be taken so seriously in the mind of a father because the obligation is law, and it will be there. You have to learn to accept it and make it a positive responsibility instead of something that you dread.

The worst thing you can do is listen to everybody else when it comes to child support. Every man that goes through it is going to have a separate story. Every man that hasn't been through it is going to have an opinion. All of them are going to be discouraging and mind-boggling. What you don't want to do is take your mind off of the big picture or the important factor; the kids need to be taken care of.

Soulja Soulja

The most common issue with fathers and child support is that the mother is not spending the money on the kids. Macho dads have the largest issue with where the dollar goes when it's already spent. They make threats to quit working, or to cause harm to the mother if all of the money isn't spent on the kids (as if these two solutions will make their lives better). They don't stop to realize that this portion of their check doesn't belong to them in the first place. Once a judge makes an order for you to pay X amount of money you are now exempt from that amount every week or month. It is no longer yours. You shouldn't worry about where it goes. When an employer pays you your wages, they don't tell you how to spend it. When you put money in other women's pockets for whatever they claim to need, you don't always check to see if she really spent the money on what she said. When anyone pays you, you do what you want with the money. Why? Because it is your money. Child support wasn't meant to go directly to kids. Otherwise child support payments would be made out to kids. It was meant to go to the custodial parent, which happens to be the mother in most cases. Good mothers spend way more money and time on the children than your once a week visits, and usually spend more on a daily basis than your once a week child support payments. You are just doing your part in assisting her. I can't stress enough to fathers that as long as the mother keeps the lights on, the water running, the transportation going, the food plentiful, and the rent paid, you don't need to ever question what she is doing with your X amount of money. It is just putting a little help here and there, which you very well should be doing. This is what women have been trying to explain all along in so many words, and this is what I am telling you is true as a father myself.

True enough, there are women that completely take advantage of the system. They don't want to work. They don't do anything to provide for themselves besides live off of you and government assistance. They continue to make babies and repeat the cycle. These types of women do make you not want to help them in any way. They also keep themselves up off of your money but have the kids looking crazy. Some spend your money on other men. All that I can say is that you should've spotted her as this type of person

12 Gauge Shotkids

before you decided to impregnate her. Maybe next time you will be more careful in your screening process. I guarantee all of those signs were there at the beginning. Your agenda may not have let you pay attention until it was too late. On the flip side, since it is too late, you can only simply keep calm first and foremost and try to explain to her how you feel and how she is taking from and neglecting the kids. This most likely won't work, but fussing and screaming at her about it and making threats definitely won't. As long as she isn't abusing the kids, you will be obligated to pay her the money. The courts won't feel sympathy for you; they will simply wonder why you made such an ignorant choice in picking a mother for your child/children. So it will do no good to go crying to them about where she is spending the money. I guess the best way of thinking about it is that if she didn't have your money to spend on the extras, your kids wouldn't even have the little that they do have now. The main focus is, first, are the kids still showing genuine happiness, are the utilities on, is the rent being paid, and are they eating properly? If you can prove these things aren't happening, then your next step is to try and prove neglect. Other than that, you chose that, and you suffer the consequences of that choice.

All of this stuff we have to deal with should be done much easier and go a lot smoother, but we have different kinds of people with whole different agendas. Mothers and fathers can really make it difficult to move peacefully through the court system. One difficult negotiation that should be much easier seems to be when it comes down to visitation.

Visitation is a necessity in parenthood. Yet, it is one that a parent will go to great measures, using trickery and lies to prevent it. Don't get bent out of shape when you are denied your parenting time. An annoying parent wants to see and hear your reaction to see if you will actually hurt yourself in the process. They know it and can hear it in your voice when you desperately want to see your children. They won't even allow you to talk to them on the phone. The next thing they want to see is if you will violate a restraining order, or vandalize, incriminate yourself, or fall victim to substance abuse. They know these things will get you a one way ticket to the lock-up with a whole other case to fight. You never want to give them that advantage over you.

Instead, you have to learn how to work the court system. Some states and counties, but definitely not all, will allow police to intervene and force parenting time when there is a court order in place. You have to negotiate visitation that works out for you though. Don't pick times that are unrealistic for your schedule, as you will be the one in contempt of court and you will look bad. Negotiate realistic times and stick to it. Some counties won't allow police to get involved with family issues to the point where they force the kids out of the house. This is because courts want to keep kids from always having to be exposed to police during disputes. This does harm children emotionally and mentally, so I do understand it. But it does cause a problem to fathers. It gives the mother more leverage to keep the kids away longer. When you file contempt hearings for her denying you parenting time it takes about six months to get into court. That is ridiculous and painful to know that you may have to go that long without seeing your kids. You just have to hold on to faith that she won't remain so cruel for too long. When you ignore her and stop calling and pressing her, when you don't let her know how much it is bothering you this usually reverses in a shorter amount of time. It is crucial that you don't play her games. It is crucial that you never show weakness. It is crucial that you stay calm at all times, especially at the beginning. When you have a game player on your hands you will start to recognize patterns and you will know when she starts the games up again.

While you are in court, be prepared. If you need to schedule a hearing for a dispute file whatever petitions and motions that you need to file. The main ones to think about are the contempt petitions, for when she denies you parenting time, and modification petitions when you need to make changes to parenting time or child support orders. The timing is crucial when it comes to filing. You want to be on top of a game player. They will try to beat you to the punch when they have conspired up a

12 Gauge Shotkids

bunch of lies to use against you. You definitely have to worry more about games and lies when she knows you are a fighter.

Being the petitioner also lets the courts see that you aren't playing about your rights, or the rights of the child. When you are the initial petitioner who gets all of the court precedings started, you remain the petitioner all through any future precedings as well, while the mother remains the respondent. This is important to know when you are filing petitions and you came to the part at the top that states whether you are the petitioner or the respondent. No matter who files what first at any time after the very first filing, you remain the petitioner. You will always be the one with the burden of proof, which is a good thing simply because you want to be able to state your facts and prove your points first before she can have the chance to tell her stories and lies. Some judges will start with whomever they choose, but starting with the petitioner is the way that it is supposed to work.

You need to make all necessary changes that you have to make when you are dealing with the courts. All of it has to be done by motions and petitions. Petitions and motions are the only way to get the court's attention. As tempting as it is to want to call and get things rolling, they will only tell you that you have to file a petition without the parties ever having to attend a court hearing. It all depends on how serious the situation is and whether or not it can be settled out of court. If the two parties can agree on something without going to court, put it in writing and have it notarized then file a motion with the courts. A judge can issue a proper order without the two parties having to show up in court in many cases. If there will be a dispute between the two parties on any situation, you can be assured that there will be a hearing to prepare for. Simple changes that deal with one of you changing an address or switching jobs or other simple orders the courts told you to follow will not have to go to court. They have to be filed though. Without filing any order a judge asked you to timely file you run the risk of losing favor with the courts and risk getting unsatisfactory judgments and orders against you. Some judges that aren't so lenient will even hold you in contempt for very simple orders that

Soulja Soulja

were either forgotten or ignored. Stay on top of what you are told to do and make all of the necessary changes that you need to make. When things are not going correctly this is the only way that you get the courts to know and intervene. Eventually the mother will get tired of you having to drag her to court and she will start to shape up. The mother or the courts aren't always used to a father that is determined and takes consistent action.

6 DEALING WITH THE COURT SYSTEM

Although going to court can produce satisfactory results when handling an out of control co-parent, it can also backfire on you and produce unsatisfactory results if you aren't conducting yourself correctly. If you aren't keeping calm and letting God work in your case you will fall down in your own hole that you dug. You have to learn how to have an extraordinary amount of patience when dealing with the court system. Without seeking God's help with your patience and attitude you wind up trying to handle problems on your own, and in your own way. As the court process may be long and hassling, taking matters that the courts don't seem to be examining or handling correctly into your own hands may seem like a more satisfying approach.

But that is exactly the route that you don't want to go. When you are in the midst of a heated dispute the mind will rarely produce the correct solutions. It will only tell you all of the wrong things that you feel you need to conspire in the midst of the battle, and will later make you feel bad for even thinking that way. If you've done what an angry mind told you to it will only satisfy you temporarily but have a lasting effect on all other parties involved, depending on how you have acted out. You want to stay away from doing devious and spiteful things to a person that will never make matters better and could make your life worse. If you can't openly discuss the resolution with a trusted source or get positive feedback from people, you may be thinking the wrong way.

When dealing with the court system staying out of trouble is the key to a satisfactory gain. This is why you have to let the wishes of the mind go and let God work. No matter how long it takes let everything work itself out. As long as you are doing all that you are supposed to be doing and fighting in all of the ways that you should, you should have all of the faith in the world that things will work out the way that they should; and that doesn't mean all of the ways that you want them too. As long as you don't give up evil should not consume your mind and soon you will see positive results.

The courts pay close attention to how you conduct yourself in court, and definitely out of court. A party's criminal history and background are heavily examined by the courts. This should not sway you from going through with the court process, but it should convince you to walk a straight and narrow path from here on out. You can have all of the proper etiquette, grammar, and mannerism in the world in front of a judge. You can portray yourself as the best dad in the world. But the second that they find out that you are out in the world getting arrested or causing problems to other people, or even yourself, all of that will go out of the window immediately. A court will not show favor to a party that is troubled. They will feel that if you are hurting yourself, or others, you will hurt the child. If you are seeking custody of your children, but are getting into trouble, you can hang it up on that idea. A court will definitely not run the risk of giving the child to the wrong parent that could possibly be embattled. The courts will not stop parenting time or interaction with the children just off of a criminal

12 Gauge Shotkids

history though, unless you have posed a risk of harming them. Other than that, you must first understand what it is that you are trying to do and how your conduct looks to the courts when considering your requests. Always take into account that they don't know you and they are only going to assume by the facts that they see more than what they are simply told.

Do the best that you can to stay out of the way of trouble. During these hard times it becomes way too easy to fall into drug and alcohol abuse. Using drugs and alcohol to block out problems are temporary fixes, but the problems worsen and they remain. Alcohol and drugs will cause a person with an uneasy mind to do and say all of the wrong things at the wrong times, all while thinking that they are doing the right things. All along they are hurting themselves and affecting their case greatly.

The impaired and intoxicated person has a higher chance of getting arrested and being in the wrong places at the wrong times. It is too easy during these times to become addicted to abusing these drugs to hide the pain and deal with feelings and emotions, so it is better to not even put yourself in danger of letting these be your downfalls. It never looks like they will be a problem at first, but they later turn into a problem, and just when your case may be going in your favor you get caught up in some kind of trouble. You don't want to risk losing your life, your freedom, and/or your children from abusing drugs and alcohol. They don't rid you of problems; they actually make problems worse. Also, you get exposed to your children as a drunk or a drug addict. It is easy to hide it at first, but once it develops into a problem everyone will see as the destruction unfolds. Your co-parent will love every moment of this and she can't wait to make the courts aware of your problems. Don't ever think that either the co-parent or the courts won't find out. As the father, the courts and the co-parent have their eyes peeled on every piece of dirt that they can find on you. They will use it on you to the very first chance they get and make you look like a horrible parent and person. It is all a strategy that is used to favor the mother and we as fathers allow it all to happen when we put ourselves at risk of getting into any trouble. This is what makes us losers in a long fought battle that we really deserve to win.

Always stay on top of what she is doing when it comes down to dealing with the courts. The courts will send you notifications of scheduled court appearances that she may have filed, or various court orders, but you need to know what it is that you need to prepare for and what she may be trying to do and say that will hurt you. Don't ever just set letters and notifications from the courts aside and ignore them. Examine them fully. Read every word, paragraph, and sentence. Stay prepared for everything that is thrown at you. One slip up can cost you a lot when fighting in a family dispute. I always tell fathers to never let a mother handle the courts on her own and he just follows her lead. There are some points when you have to take initiative as a father. We now understand that we have no rights to a child without establishing paternity first. We also know that by establishing paternity that we are now going to be committed to a child support order. This is going to happen unless the mother isn't getting government assistance and suggests the courts don't make you pay, which very rarely happens. So since you know this will happen, why not be the petitioner that requests that paternity be established and a child support order be established. It is going to happen anyway. The problem with fathers is that we want to cut a corner or two by remaining silent, but end up creating a much bigger issue anyway. One of the most common issues is how fathers handle child support. Most fathers still have no clue how child support is calculated, nor do they realize how their lack of involvement puts them at risk of paying outrageous child support payments.

In most states, child support is calculated by how much you get paid, but also subtracted by how often you have overnights with your children in a calendar year. Most fathers are confused or don't have any clue about these calculations because they always allow the mother to go put them on child support while they aren't anywhere around. This is where fathers make the biggest mistake at. Naturally, if a father has no reported income, or job, the courts will issue a minimum child support payment order. The problem

12 Gauge Shotkids

lies in the hands of the father that does have a job and a good paying job at that. If this father allows the mother to go in front of the clerk that is calculating the payment and give them all of his information by herself, then he is in trouble. She will most likely tell the clerk that he only sees the children on weekends, if she even mentions that he sees them at all. She will state that she has all of the overnights. She will say that he doesn't pay her any kind of support. When the courts find this information out, plus they find out how much he gets paid and how often he works, he will surely pay the maximum payment the court can order. If he was actually there to tell the courts how often he really had overnights with his children, he wouldn't be ordered to pay so much, no matter how much he gets paid or how often he works. Most fathers don't know this. The amount of overnights subtracts your payment obligation. It makes sense because if you have the children overnight for half the year then you have an equal amount of expense as she does from the children. You will owe much less for your obligation to the children. When a father is present most courts will feel less of a need to check to see how much you get paid and/or how often you work. You can tell them you work part-time when you really work full-time. I don't suggest lying to the courts, but I am trying to stress to you how being present and involved in all precedings will benefit you in more ways than you know. If you aren't involved she will tell them all of the worse things that she can and they will listen to all of it. When a father receives his obligation in the mail he is upset and angry at the judge when he is the one that let the co-parent give them all of the information without ever disputing anything beforehand. Most mothers won't even lie nor be able to dispute what they know is true about your parenting time when you are right there with her in the clerk's office. It is when you aren't present that they make up anything to get that big check. Then you are stuck with the large and outrageous payment. But you let her do all of the work and all of the talking so you pay the price. If you did happen to go about the situation in this way don't be alarmed. You can still file petitions and get your facts to the courts. File a modification of child support petition and schedule a hearing that will allow you to be treated fairly. Arguing at her and being angry at the judge won't cut it though. You have to get yourself involved.

Everyone doesn't have the time or the drive to stay up with the case or learn for themselves about their case. Doing so is very tiresome and overwhelming at times. Fathers that don't see immediate results will find themselves wanting to give up or cause the co-parent some serious problems. This is because everyone doesn't comprehend the same or as fast as the next. When dealing with the courts, all that you have to keep you active and sane are hope and faith. You lose either of these you start to spiral out of control in the mind. So you have to decide how you are going to fight.

In family court, some parties find it much easier to fight with a lawyer. A lawyer takes the pressures of tedious researching and large amounts of time spent stressing and fighting out of your equation. They are more knowledgeable of your rights and your child's rights. They file your motions and petitions for you. They help you plan and think about the right steps to take. A lawyer will speak for you. They are everything that you need to accomplish what you need to accomplish. They come at a hefty price though. It is almost like paying to get your driver's license back though. It is most definitely worth it, and having your children grow up the right way with their rights being enforced is priceless. A lawyer knows how to deal with a judge and the right words to say. They are very familiar with the terminology used in court. If you are short of the mind and/or tongue, a lawyer is the best way to represent yourself in this matter. At least you can discuss with them what is currently taking place and they can immediately jump on it, knowing exactly what to say and do to produce the right gain. A lawyer really provides a piece of mind. They don't stop you from doing at least some work, but a great deal of it they are being paid to do for you. Neither are they able to achieve all of the results that you expect. You still have to remain clean and free of troubles to make a lawyers representation on your behalf work. You still can fail the whole mission due to your conduct. A lawyer should be up front with you on what to expect in every step of your

12 Gauge Shotkids

developing case. Never expect perfection and never expect to be able to just kick your feet up. Your co-parent will still drag you through problems and you still feel pains as results of her actions. Help your lawyer, since this is your situation. Enlighten them on new events, and don't just let them do everything either. What you don't tell them they won't know.

Most fathers choose to represent themselves. This is called representing 'pro se,' or self. Representing 'pro se' is not looked down upon so much in family court, but it can produce unsatisfactory results depending on how complex the case is. A case where two parties are mostly in agreement has better success at representing 'pro se.' The courts easily take their ideas and suggestions into consideration better and issue orders accordingly based off of the agreements. When two parties are involved in heated battles, representing 'pro se' is much less desirable to the courts and eventually to the parties involved. It is just too much back and forth and far too much disagreement that the courts would rather lawyers were mediating the case. They would rather have attorneys to communicate with than two angry and bitter parents. These kinds of parties waste far too much court time and are rarely ever prepared to resolve disagreements. They drag on hours at a time, court appearance after appearance, and nothing ever seems to get resolved.

The parties are free to do everything pro se though. It is your constitutional right. It is also free of charge. A judge has no choice but to schedule you and hear you out. You have the burden of speaking for yourself and producing your own case though. You have to do your own research. You have to prepare yourself. You will be treated by the book and the courts will expect that you know how to handle your case, the courts, and know your rights the very first time. They won't show mercy to you just because you don't understand something. You file 'pro se' you must know exactly what you are doing and what to do and say to that judge. A judge's favorite words to an uneducated party are "you should seek legal counsel." So do yourself a favor and know what you are talking about and what you're doing. A judge knows how to play you and go completely over your head because they know way more about the law than you. If your case is too complex, don't try to go heads up with a judge unless you are confident that you know what you are doing. It is smart to start off initial precedings like paternity, child support, and visitation pro se. But if the case gets more complex than that seek a lawyer asap. If a judge happens to issue a guardian ad litem on your case, to mediate, start putting your money together and seek legal counsel. A guardian ad litem is similar to a public defender in a criminal case. They work for the state and they dig for information that will make your case harder. They usually side with the custodial parent and they come down harder on the other parent. If a guardian ad litem is appointed, that is an indicator that your case is getting too complex. Guardian ad litem's claim to work for the child, but they don't even get to know the child in most cases; they take very little interest in you as a father (non-custodial parent) no matter what they say. Don't trust them; it's time to get your own lawyer.

The judge is the one that you ultimately have to worry about. This is the one that you have to impress. As hard as it is for most people dealing with difficult cases, the judge is the one that you have to keep your cool with. They make life changing decisions that are sometime unpredictable, and some that will piss you completely off too. But when it is all said and done, your demeanor, attitude, and conduct will show the most to the judge that is presiding over your case. You don't want to lose their favor at any time.

The judge has the difficult task of determining which parent the child is most well off with, who is lying, and what arrangements will best suit the child. Parents that disagree all the time and stay trying to hurt one another make the judge have to do too much intervention that neither party will like in the end. A judge's only concern is for the well being of the child, so both parents bickering back and forth will mean absolutely nothing to the judge, and will in turn make the parents look and feel stupid and immature. The judge wants the parents to get along and agree for the sake of the children. This angers the judge when they constantly see two people fighting over and over. Someone, or both parents, is going

12 Gauge Shotkids

to suffer for wasting the court's time. Parents think that showing anger for and revealing and exposing a co-parent's history of thinking or actions will better their chances at success. While it is taken into account and record, it really does the opposite and makes both parties look bad. A judge can look at the relationship history and see if there was a time when the two weren't so heated. They can tell if at one point they loved each other. They can use all of this to tell who is trying to hurt who. They can tell who does or doesn't have the child's best interest in mind. This is all that they care about when making decisions. Like it was mentioned before, all of the anger and bickering just gives them a negative image of you and makes you look bad. The judge is used to dealing professionally with attorneys, so having to deal with unprofessional, angry parents doesn't align correctly with what their career description describes, so they tend to become more impatient and uncomfortable with these types of parents.

Some fathers hurt themselves by carrying their anger for the co-parent into the court room and lashing out at the judge. This is the quickest way to lose everything you've worked hard for. This is a complete no-no. Although the times may be extremely hard and different for you, the judge is not to blame. They are merely there to help resolve what two parents can't seem to resolve on their own. When you are uneducated and/or unprepared you have to expect that there will be unsatisfactory results. The courts are not designed to be taken on by the layman. You must know that the judge may do and say things that could throw you off of your square, but you must remain level-headed and calm. They want to be able to see if you are as crazy as your co-parent has been telling them or not. They want to prove if you know what it takes to successfully make it through the case without first snapping out or exploding. They want to see if you are violent in nature, verbally abusive, or if you play games. This lets them see what type of person you really are and also what type of person you may show your kids that you are. Snapping out in front of a judge is closely examined and highly not recommended. You must remember that they can see or hear about all of the positive things that you do or are about, but the second that they see or hear anything negative it will outweigh anything positive. You may even be dealing with a biased judge that only pays attention to the mother and doesn't seem to honor any of your testimony, but you should still remain calm. In this case, God will expose her before you get a chance to successfully prove anything. You just have to trust and believe that He will deal with her, and just like you He wants the best for your children as well. He may just be allowing her to act like this for a while to build a successful case for you. Deceitful, lying, guilty parties end up hurting themselves over time and the truth comes out. So even when it seems the judge is taking sides, remain positive and remain right and you will end up prevailing. These judges don't know you nor do they love or like you. They don't even know all that is wrong in your case. They only know what they see and hear. Deal with the judge respectfully, courteously, and professionally at all times no matter what you think of them. It won't make your life any better by acting or talking crazy. It makes your case worse, as the judge has the final say. They recognize when you've acted professionally and they may have acted harshly. They can make their actions right before you can make yours right.

Always remember to document everything. Make police reports for missed parenting time by calling into the police station instead of calling them out to you. Note the report number and go purchase the report from the station. Make note of harassing or disturbing phone calls and/or texts. Make note of all events that pertain to the case. Even keep a calendar of all the days that you do have your scheduled visitation. This documentation saves all kinds of back and forth disputing when you get to court. The one that has the documentation looks great to the judge too. This is the person that they believe most. They go off of proven facts, not hearsay. Documenting shows how involved you are and how important the resolution of your case is to you. It is a way of showing consistency, responsibility, and initiative on your part. These are all of the qualities that you want a judge to notice about you. The key to it is to remain smart about everything that you do and you shouldn't have too many issues dealing with them. Things will definitely start to go your way. Just don't allow the process to

12 Gauge Shotkids

discourage you overall, because it can be a little weird when you haven't been through anything like that before.

7 WHY DOES SHE HATE ME

"But why does she hate me anyway?" "What did I really do that was so bad?" "Why is she still hateful and bitter after so long?" "Why can't we just get along?" "Will this battle ever end?" "Will the drama ever end?" "Why can't we be friends at least for the sake of the kids?"

Any true, loving father would be asking all of the same questions if he had any kind of real concern for his and his children's lives and futures. Even while showing unbelievable amounts of strength, just because you have to, the questions and the plotting of peaceful resolutions never cease. You always want to know why she hates you so much. Or does she even really hate you at all? Is this just a vengeful and spiteful battle that you are caught up in? She probably doesn't even hate you at all. She probably just wants to hurt you like she may claim that you hurt her.

You can always start by apologizing for what you have done to hurt her in the past. You may have done this before but this time

12 Gauge Shotkids

you need to really mean it. Once she has gone too far in the games then apologizing doesn't even seem to work. It is a possibility that she has also made some messed up decisions when separating the family that she is now regretting. This makes it easier for her to attack you without thinking about the consequences for her actions. Most young women that have grown up submitting to a particular man, and never quite experiencing their own independence, usually will take a step out on their own at some point and at any cost. The problem is that it is mostly for selfish reasons. And when you bring children into the world you are obligated to those children's needs as well. Just because you want to experience life on your own that doesn't take away the fact that the kids still need their mother to be stable at all times, and it definitely doesn't mean that you should risk struggling just because you want to prove something to the father of the kids. It is not all about you anymore once you have even just one child. All thoughts and all actions have to surround the well being of the child as well. This means that it can't be that easy to just up and leave anymore. This doesn't include households that are violent or in any way abusive. This is for the ones that want to have experiences with other people and those that just simply want to do for themselves. It is not that easy anymore when you have children. All of these fantasies and lifestyles should be well thought out and acted upon before making children. That goes for mothers and fathers. Children deserve to have both parents in the household that love them and guide them together. When a mother breaks up a household for unnecessary, selfish reasons it is not very long before the backlash comes back to bite her. But it's the same thing for fathers too.

Let's just say, for example, that she left you for another man that she should've never allowed herself to be involved with in the first place. True enough, it always starts out good and feels good. Listening to words without seeing immediate action can also make the grass look greener on the other side. But what about when she starts to see that this man is either no better and/or far less than what she expected? What about when she realizes that she just messed up her family life for someone who is not worth it and is not going to last another minute? Women fail to realize sometime

Soulja Soulja

how convincing a snake can be at first. She doesn't think about why this man that barely even knows her is so eager for her to come with him and help ruin her family. They don't think about what this man's agenda could really be. All of these things start to really unfold once all of the damage has been done. Another thing that they so poorly miss before they make multiple life-changing decisions is the obvious fact that when they did creep around with this mysterious man the children were either never or rarely around. This man is only interested in her, because he doesn't know her children enough to have any kind of interest in them. She has no idea how he will really react or want to be involved with her children on a full time basis. This may be discussed but it is not seen. And plus a snake will say anything to get his wishes or desires fulfilled. I call them snakes because I don't think that any man should have a desire or intent to break up a home. It takes too much to build a home, and even more to maintain it and keep it happy. Women become more vulnerable at any time she feels any unhappiness in the household. The weaker ones will make themselves available to the world in an attempt to discover what she may come across. If in fact it does lead to her ending a relationship and going into another man's arms, she usually doesn't experience better results. She experiences shame and guilt. She experiences regret. She has to stare at her children and wonder why she did what she did, and in turn try to do something to make herself feel better. This is when it is better to attack you and pull out and pull up anything she can to make you look and feel bad. She becomes lost in her own mess that she created. It's not your fault but she wouldn't dare place all of the blame on herself. She has to dig into the past and bring back old feelings that hurt and upset her before and make those same feelings come back to haunt you. This is why you have a hard time understanding her motives to outburst and do the things that she does. She is trying to find a way to cope with her own misfortunes. Because we all understand what happens to people that make the wrong decisions; they have to deal with the consequences of their actions. And when you hurt children, or you mess up families due to your own agendas and/or selfishness, you have hell to pay for that. The crazy thing is you can see their suffering and crumbling even while they try to prove

12 Gauge Shotkids

to you that they are so content and proud of themselves. Everything but contention shows though. She no longer wants to see you happy. It's amazing how a person can go out and make the mistake of destroying a salvageable family for their own agenda and gain but turn around and be the one unhappy. The one that was left in the dust is the one that picks themselves up and turns out the happiest. You would think that the person that chases after their own happiness would be the one that is the winner, but they wind up playing themselves. So when this happens it creates bitterness and rage. It pains them to see you able to make it through without them. Your pleasure becomes their pain.

It can get crazy when you are dealing with someone who once had the proper sight but allowed themselves to be taken over and misguided by someone else. What would make a person think that they would pick up skills elsewhere that they never even tried to gain with the one they were with? People don't realize that you can have the one that you are with the same way as the ones that you chase in many cases. You do have people that actually do want someone that is a downgrade from what they have already, and it is and should be impossible to get a person to downgrade themselves for anyone. For example, a woman may have a hard working man but she has a strong desire for a petty dealer or street hustler. Or she may have a man that has changed from a street thinker but she wants a man that is involved with the streets. Then when she gets him she realizes that she actually had it better with who she had before. She may be a little misguided and lost on what life she thinks is better for her. The only way she can know is to go out and see for herself though. It never will give her the satisfaction that she desires. When God puts a family together He wants that family to work. It is intended to come with problems that will later result in growth, which every family is expected to achieve. When you make choices to destroy a family that God put together believe that that is your choice and your choice only. You have to deal with the consequences of that choice.

A person that can't stand to see you happy will do any amount of things to destroy your happiness. You don't want to flaunt in front

Soulja Soulja

of this person. It is way too easy for them to hope and plot on the worse for you. You can tell when you are dealing with this type of person when they constantly put you down and always try to get in the way of your progression. The best way a mother can get in the way is by using your kids as weapons and doing whatever they can to see you get into trouble. Be careful when dealing with restraining orders and when getting into arguments. Arguments with a co-parent can make the whole rest of your day miserable. They will say and do things to anger you with hopes that they can get you to react in a way that will lead to your arrest or destruction. The wrong actions can lead to years of unhappiness for you and overall it will be your fault in the end. What is not clearly understood is that when the mother is unhappy the father is unhappy and the children will be unhappy as well. You have to do your very best to not let anyone steal your joy because when someone is playing with your kids it is extremely easy to fall into their traps. Not only that, you give them power over you and your emotions.

You may be experiencing problems out of her because secretly she wants you back too. She may have feelings for you still but don't feel comfortable expressing that to you. If she is shameful for the things that she has done to you she will definitely be reluctant to let you in her world knowing that you have a higher chance of rejecting her and her wishes.

Don't think that just because she says it's over, or does hateful and spiteful things to you, that that is her true self and true feelings spilling out onto you. Most times it is everything but that. When you have shared a true love at some point, a real chemistry, when you and her have been through ups and downs and shared deep intimacy together, you should never think that just because one has a change of heart that they have completely lost all of their love and feelings of care and concern for you. Instead, these true feelings are hard fought and are constantly interrupted to try and only display what the person wants to show on the outside and to themselves and the outside world. All along they really want to have you back in the way that they had you before, if not better.

12 Gauge Shotkids

How could she ever express that to you though? Do you remember when you were in grade school and the boy that liked the girl always did something or said something mean to her just about every time he seen her? All along everyone knew that he secretly liked her. She was always on his mind and he had to do something to disturb her. This is the same way that women prey on men when they still hold secret feelings for him but have no other ways at getting his attention. They find themselves conspiring to do very mean things to him as well. They want to hurt him just to know that they are the ones that caused the pain. As long as she knows that she has to be on his mind because she is the cause of his suffering she gets a pleasure from that. She plays the devil in his life by torturing him over and over again, but definitely not killing him. She would rather see his pain.

The last thing that she is going to do is let him know that she is still in love. She will do anything to not reveal that she made a mistake by destroying the family. Her shame and her guilt will not give you any satisfaction of knowing what she really feels. Even if you are not playing her games with her she must still keep up at her pace to keep her from softening up on you and possibly revealing how she truly feels. All that you get out of her is the devilish woman that you can't understand anymore. You will retract events over and over in your mind, but will never figure out why she hates you so much.

But she really doesn't hate you; she loves you. She doesn't want to see you dead. She just wants to see you hurt a little like she is hurting. She would do anything to take back her initial moves and have the relationship back together. But she has done so many evil things to you that there is possibly no way in hell that you could think of taking her back. She has revealed so much of what type of mean and spiteful person that she can be that there is no way that you could possibly want that in your life. And sadly she knows all of this. She can see that you have moved on, probably have a good lady and a good relationship going, and she knows you aren't leaving you new life for her especially considering all that she has been putting you through. All while playing the game she never

Soulja Soulja

thought about the Plan B if the Plan A wasn't what she expected it to be. The objective is to destroy. It isn't for you to simply heal after a day or so. If she puts restraining orders on you she expects you to go to jail with a case to fight in whatever way that you can mess up. If she takes the kids from you the objective is for you to hurt yourself through doing things out of anger and ruining your mind, body, and soul with harmful substances and/or actions. She could just simply want you to give up and walk out of your children's lives. She doesn't expect that you won't fall into these traps. When these Plan A's don't work the way that she intended them to she angrily moves to another plan. Now time has gone by and she has played game after game. All of them were felt but none of them got the best of you. All the while she has seen your endurance, she has seen how you've still progressed and she still has to fight the fact that she can't shake the love that she has for you. You may think to yourself, 'how can someone that loves me do me so wrong?' You would be amazed at the lengths a person that loves you would go to punish you to keep you under their control.

So how do they react when they realize that they can't win? How do they soften up on you without seeming anything less that victorious? What can she do when she knows that she has done so much to hurt you? All that she can do now is wallow in her own shame and regret. That's why people should watch what they do to other people. The time will come back when you have to live with your consequences of your actions. If you can't, or aren't going to kill a person, why try to break them over and over? You still have to face that person. Who wants to have to face a person that they have tried to hurt over and over? Who wants to have to live with that regret for the rest of their life and pay for it when they have to look into that person's eyes? That is especially a person that you have to interact with because they are a co-parent to your child. Hard feelings don't last forever and a person can forgive what another has done to them, but they don't forget that easily. Now the damage is done, the feelings are painfully intensified, and there seems to be nothing that can be said to make things right or even better. A person is now completely out of trust and totally on edge

12 Gauge Shotkids

waiting on what game is going to be played next. So now whatever secret feelings a person has must remain just that, a secret. And it's hard to hold in boxed up feelings, but it is all a consequence of playing so many devilish games that it became impossible to win back the heart of someone that you loved all along.

A person that is done with you won't possess hatred and anger for you when you didn't abuse them physically, mentally, or emotionally. Even if you did, they would be so content with being away from you that hatred and anger would come second to joy and happiness. When someone is done, and completely done with you, they don't want to have control over you. They don't want to play little games with you or your children. They want you out of their life. They don't care who you are with. They don't want to argue. They don't prey on your downfall. You don't worry about these things from someone who is done with you. It is only the ones that have some kind of love and feelings that they are hanging onto. It is not that easy for someone to pick up and leave no matter what decisions they've made. You may be all that they've known for some years now, so they have to find something to do with what they feel. And when it is not going as sweet as they've wanted it to, expect it to go sour.

Boyfriends, family members, and friends play a big part in why they've made their decisions and why they react the way they react as well. When one lets these members make suggestions for them it can cause the main two people that need to be in compliance with one another to fall apart. Most new boyfriends never have the best interest of the kids, and definitely the father, in mind. They are only thinking about the woman going back to their ex. They want to steer her feelings as far away from her ex as possible. This includes poisoning her mind with whatever he can to make matters worse. The best place for new boyfriends to be is out of the way. They have no clue about the history of the relationship, or the future of it. All that they go off of is what the woman tells them; and that won't be nearly enough correct information. So they should stay out. When a boyfriend gets in her ear, this is where the woman stops doing logical thinking. She is bringing in an outsider

Soulja Soulja

that is speculating with very minimal observation of the true happenings of the relationship. If she is a weaker-type woman, her actions will be based mostly off of what she can do to satisfy him. She has to hide her true feelings to make him feel like he has the upper hand.

It's the same with family members. Some are very influential. A woman's mother and father can secretly be conspiring on you as well. You hardly ever know who is in a woman's ear that is encouraging her to do certain things that you know to be completely out of her character. The fact is that if it is out of her character, something or someone is helping her think of doing strange things. You have to be leery of that cousin or that parent that may have given you the funny looks or acted strange around you. There isn't anything you can do about who is saying what, but at least you know who your real enemy is. When certain ones don't have their own lives in order they don't care about hurting another person's life. They influence all kinds of negative behavior, and the person that has to suffer the backlash and the consequences of acting out on what they influence is the person that they are influencing. See, a person may tell you that you won't hurt yourself by jumping off of the bridge, but once you trust them and you jump off of the bridge, you actually do end up hurting yourself despite what they said. The person giving all of the advice doesn't suffer at all for what they advised you to do.

The boyfriends, the family, and the friends are the ones to watch out for. They are the ones that don't really care anything about you, your relationship with your children, or any outcomes for that matter. Nor do they have to deal with anything. They don't really care. And a woman that is enraged will take whatever advice that she can from them. They may have went through similar situations before and may be encouraging behaviors that may have worked on who they were trying to hurt, but that doesn't mean that they will or have to have the same effects and outcomes for your situation. It is your job to make sure that they don't either. Misery loves company and only miserable people encourage negative

12 Gauge Shotkids

behaviors that can wind up hurting the person that they are encouraging. That is the children and the children's father.

8 CONTROLLING YOUR ANGER AND HER BITTERNESS

The games may be played for years to come. The anger and bitterness may linger around for years. Peace may not even be in sight for many years. But eventually it does come. With the right approach to her attitudes, and the willingness to be a good partner with her, the long, dark tunnel will reveal some light at the end. It takes much patience, much tongue biting, and much endurance of pain to achieve satisfactory results. As long as you don't give up on keeping a positive attitude and good behavior you will notice the changes after a while. Remember, it doesn't end until she has exhausted all possible ways of getting under your skin.

I mentioned before how even though she pretends to be so much better and well off, it is plain as day to see how much she is crumbling at the same time. And even though now you can tell that she really just has this undying love and concern for you, you can't

12 Gauge Shotkids

make it obvious to her that you actually see her as the weaker person that she is. You have to just remain in the cut and use what you now understand as your own personal strengths. Now, none of what she does should stand a chance at taking you down. Your mindset should be able to switch from, 'will this ever end' to 'this will end soon.' The way you perceive what is going on around you will greatly affect the outcomes. When you expect the worse all of the time, you will get the worse. When you expect things will turn in your favor to benefit you and your children's sake, they will do that too. Do everything, and feel all of the necessary ways that you need to so that you can produce positive feelings and outcomes.

Ways to notice that her world is falling in on her is when she produces great amounts of anger at unusual times and for unusual reasons. She can't have regular conversations with you without picking an argument. She says extreme words like 'I wish you were dead' or she threatens you with bodily harm. She can't keep up on her bills. She loses her jobs. The new boyfriend that she left you for turned out to be a bad move. She appears to be struggling. All of her misfortunes she blames you for and takes it out on you and your kids.

There could be a number of ways to notice her demise but refrain from letting that be your pleasure. The way to end the battle sooner than later is to be considerate. Always show that you care and you are not laughing at her downfalls. This only makes her want to see you down and out even more. This is not what you want or need. It is not good for the kids either. Showing that you are more concerned than pleasured by her downfalls will let her see that you believe her well being is important, which it very much so is. Although deep down you are seeing all that is caving in on her, and having a secret giggle about it, keep in mind that when she is messed up the kids will be to. If she can't pay her bills, the kids go without. If she is miserable, the kids don't get the love and attention that they deserve to have. Displaying that you are a bigger person will keep a lot of pressure off of you and it will make you a much better person. This is all that you should have a desire to be. This old game is mostly played by new players that

Soulja Soulja

equally take turns being the aggressor. Each player takes turns laughing and pointing at the other ones downfalls. Each player wants to be ahead of the next one. When one bumps the other they move ahead of them. The problem with that is that the game never ends. It just keeps going, with all players being the losers. There is no prize at the end, just hard feelings and regrets. A person's weaknesses and downfalls are a cause of what they've done to themselves. They are a cause of what they need to learn to get to a better level than what they've been on. They are intended to help them realize they have been playing the game wrong. What better way to throw them off from discovering their wrongdoings than to point and laugh at them. Now they just want to keep hiding the issues from who they see is paying attention and never get to the resolution. They now are focused on disguising the problem which is exactly what you didn't need to happen. But if pleasing your own ego is what is more important to you then you won't even realize that you can stunt her growth by using her issues as your entertainment. You unknowingly produce the opposite results. She won't get better; she will constantly try to prove to you that you were wrong about what you could clearly see.

It is not your place to judge. Both players want to be the winner, but how you go about winning is the key. It is strategic. Anything that is done deviously is going to backfire on you. But you will not notice it because the games go on. When you strategize correctly and positively you will end up getting the answers you were looking for anyway. You will have given that person the fair chance of seeing for themselves, and learning for themselves, without you causing them any further embarrassment.

If you discover for her she won't let you in. But if you let her discover for herself she may let you in. If she does, try to find a way for her to come out of her rut. Show her that you really do care. When you made the family you became obligated to the family. Do whatever that you can to help that family come up. When she is showing how lost and misguided that she really is she may need you to guide her still. You can't force this guidance on her, but if she seeks it, help her out. She may have found out that

12 Gauge Shotkids

she isn't as independent or as strong as she thought. And although the two of you aren't together anymore, your input may still be as beneficial as it used to be due to the fact that you have had the chance to know her best. If she valued your opinions and logic before there should be no reason that she wouldn't value it now. This can be a good way of turning bad feelings into good feelings. When you see that someone cares it can overturn a messy situation.

Helping her come up is also a way of controlling your anger toward the situation. It gives you a way of being involved in your family's life. It makes your input relevant. It helps you stay as strong as you can. The last thing you would want is a co-parent that you know can't handle what they are trying to do correctly, or responsibly, trying to do things on their own. This puts the children at risk of being caught up in unnecessary problems. A father that is aggressive and controlling usually is the one that experiences this type of co-parent. It's the co-parent that is tired of doing everything that you want them to do. They are tired of listening to everything that you say. They are tired of feeling like they are being controlled. You have to learn to simply suggest thoughts and ideas, instead of forcing them on her. This is sometime the whole reason a woman left to be on her own in the first place. Once you do get out of her ear she may come back to your thoughts, ideas, and opinions if she happens to need them. Many submissive women may have forgotten what it was like to think on their own, if they ever have at all. This doesn't mean that you are telling her wrong; it just means that she has more desire to use her own mind and this is how she needs to do it. You can't fault her for that. It can only lead to you dealing with a more elevated self-thinker in the future that now has her own choice of bright ideas. This is especially good when you were the only one in the relationship making all of the decisions. The two of you were always used to acting on the ideas of one mind. While you are apart you want her to learn how to think and make good decisions for herself. This could only lead to a better life for the children. Staying out of her way and letting her make these changes are ways that you are helping her become a better person.

Soulja Soulja

Another way that you control your anger is by ending all of the arguments. All of the traps that draw you into an argument have to be sought out and destroyed. The back and forth bickering will last for years to come when you give her power to pull the strings that she knows will send you into overdrive. The best way to keep fueling a fire and to keep digging a deeper and deeper hole is to keep arguing.

Arguing while you are hurt and angry with a person will never produce positive results. It only keeps the anger going and can lead to more intense negative feelings. The way to end the arguments is to seek out what she is doing or saying that causes you to get irate whenever she wants you to. It is something she knows will throw off the rest of your day. Once you figure this out you will have learned how to beat her at her own game.

It is easy to fall into an argument with her because true enough you are just as angry as her. You also have things you want to say and points that you want to get across to her as well. Like I said before, it is all a game. There is no limit to the amount of negativity that the two of you can spew into one another's lives. Every time you think of her, and vice versa, you can think of a thousand things you want to say to her to hurt her or make her think. But no matter how much of it comes out it just digs a deeper hole that never seems to end. The main objective you should be going for when dealing with an unruly co-parent is peace. You want to get along. You want to do all of this, not only for you, but for the sake of your children. Arguing constantly back and forth does everything but bring the peace that you need to be enjoying.

So once you've figured out the trigger, lock it. No longer allow her to make you pissed off and enraged by that weapon again. Once she gets on that level again it will be funny because you recognize that this is what she uses over and over to control your emotions. Either change the subject immediately without getting angry, hang up the phone peacefully, or leave. Don't stick around for a second to engage in any kind of battle. Spin off on any signs of an argument brewing up. When you can't hear words she is trying to

12 Gauge Shotkids

hurt you with they can't kill you. They can't even have a chance at messing up your day. What's even better, she will eventually figure out that you are done arguing with her. It gets old when both people have said everything they can possibly say but the arguing persists. The one that keeps up all of the fussing is usually the one with the problem.

All of the arguing is no good for the kids either. Children only want to see their parents get along. They don't need to be dragged in the middle of any kind of problems between their parents, and their ears are always open. In fact, to change the course of any conversation between you and the co-parent, keep all talks strictly about the children. When you make comments about the other parent's personal life or the way they are handling themselves, you open the door for objection and argument. None of those things should concern you more than what is going on with your children. Although you may care or have some concerns, if your intervention only leads to arguing and no resolution, then it is probably best that you stay out of it. If it is something she needs to see or learn she will experience that for herself. You getting involved will only make her act out in the worst possible way just to get under your skin. She doesn't need to feel like you are always judging her and challenging her. It will always lead to a battle.

Arguing is just a waste of time period. When you want to be on good terms it puts you right back on bad terms. When things were going good one argument heats everything back up. The bigger person will refrain from arguing back and forth at all costs. There will be disagreements that need to be sorted out, but when it ends with shots fired for personal reasons, and name calling, someone has deeper issues and isn't acting as a responsible adult or parent. Once you end all of the back and forth, she may keep trying to press you to see if you will slip but she will also be the only one angry when she realizes that she has no one to argue with her. It's ugly when you have to argue with yourself because the other stopped listening.

Soulja Soulja

The 'boyfriend' issue is a topic that needs a little more elaboration, as it is the most common reason that a man finds it harder to let go of a woman even after the relationship has been dead for some time. The thought of another man being involved with her and your children is gut wrenching at times. You may not even want her that much but hate to see her happy with anyone else. You may be content with your relationship with your children but hate the thought of them recognizing another man as a father figure. All of these thoughts are very normal and very difficult to deal with. The way that you deal with the 'new boyfriend' being around is going to be the key to how you control your anger and your emotions; and how effective you are at moving on with your life quicker and easier.

First off, you must understand that her life no longer revolves around you. Just like you are interested in other women, she is interested in other men. I can understand that you may be concerned with what kind of man is around your children, but don't think of her having someone else as a bad thing. Think of it as a bad thing if she ran the streets chasing man after man and bringing all of these men around your children. It is bad if she is out being a whore and constantly putting the party life and the street life over her children. When a woman has 'a boyfriend' she is usually pretty grounded and not out trying to see how many dates she can find. Most men will start to complain about a 'new boyfriend' doing this and that in front of the kids when they do or have done the exact same things in front of them. None of it is good, but who are you to judge? You have to trust that she won't allow a harmful or abusive person into her life or the children's lives. Responsible mothers will screen 'new boyfriends' much better than you would think. They know what they don't want around their children and they will rid it from them when they feel the need to. What they do discover about a 'new boyfriend' you will never know it unless she feels comfortable enough talking to you, or maybe in the aftermath. Either way, just know that she is paying way more attention than you ever could.

12 Gauge Shotkids

What you can't help but notice is when the guy turns out to be pretty decent. When the children like him, when you can't find any issues with him, and when time has gone by and the two of them are still together, you should probably worry less. All that really matters is that the man isn't mistreating the kids and that he is a good father figure. What you have to understand is that it is not at all a bad thing for kids to have two fathers. Don't confuse it with the kids not recognizing you for who you are, because that could never happen to an actively involved dad, nor do the kids want anyone to take your place. Imagine if you had two fathers. Two men to teach you how to be a man. Two men that give you two different perspectives on life. Two men that love you and protect you and want to see you succeed. That alone can turn a child into a brilliant person. It is all about how you perceive the situation. You can't sit around and expect the worse all of the time. It won't change what is meant to happen regardless. If this is the life those children are supposed to have it will be that way. You will see that later and will feel bad for treating the situation so negatively.

If you don't want her, let her go. It is her life and her body. You can't and won't control that. You will only wind up hurting yourself over it. If you do have feelings for her and do want her back, you still have to let her go and possibly if you hold on to the attraction she may find her way back to you as long as you aren't pressing and stressing her. 'New boyfriends' rarely turn into long term relationships. She will always know who she can go back to if that is what you want her to do, and that ends up being what she wants to do. It's crazy how we as fathers can create such a stir over someone that we don't even know, or just because we have strange feelings about them and/or secret agendas. What those two have going on may not even last a minute. She may be going through a short phase, or even at the beginning of a long journey to find what and who it is she really needs. She may wind up right back with you or not. Either way, as long as the children are happy and treated respectfully there is nothing to worry about. The mind can conjure all types of negativity that will have nothing to do with the situation. Also, be careful of what you think up. You may watch it come true if you think it into existence enough. You should want

Soulja Soulja

to think of everything going good. You should want to encourage the mother of your children to be careful to seek out positive people, and the importance of doing so for the children. Also, continue to trust that she is smart and responsible enough to do just that, even when you are not all in her ear forcing her to pay attention to it.

This brings up an interesting point. It is about how important it is to stay positive throughout the whole ordeal. Positivity displays great character and relieves tons of stress. It isn't always easy to stay positive, but boy does doing so produce some of the best results that you couldn't even think up on your own. It makes total sense that thinking negatively brings negative results and thinking positively brings positive results. It all starts with the thoughts. The first thing we do on both ends is start thinking on what kind of result that this action would bring. If it is a negative action it either hurts or angers the other person. If it is a positive action it either creates a peaceful resolution, or at least something both people can live with.

But when you are engaged in battle who is thinking of what it takes to make both people's lives better? Who isn't thinking about how to hurt the other, especially when the other person is constantly launching grenades in their direction? All that consumes the minds are negative thoughts, over and over again. The positive thinker would constantly remind themselves that there will be positive results in the end. The positive thinker would understand that they are going to have to take some hard shots in the midst of a heated battle. But the battle can't stay heated for long, as long as they aren't helping to fuel the fire, thus causing more heat on top of an already heated situation. The positive thinker will be the most strategic soldier involved in the war. They can see the plots and plans before and as soon as they are attempted. They are prepared by recapping on past events and strategies used previously to bring them down. They aren't surprised, nor are they impressed by shots fired at them. Although it is possible to get under a positive person's skin, you can't throw them off so easily.

12 Gauge Shotkids

You want her to see that she can't bring you down, and that you aren't going to get yourself worked up trying to battle her. When she sees that you remain proud, happy, positive, and undefeated she will follow suit. When you fight the fire with the fire you get a huge blaze. But when you fight the fire with water, you put out the fire. And a resistant fire will burn for longer than expected, but it will die away slowly until it is completely extinguished. She can't help but react the way that you are reacting. You have to think, 'why would she be motivated to be so mean if I'm not?' You have to wonder, 'if I was to stop giving her my valuable time by debating and arguing and feuding, wouldn't I feel better and wouldn't she most likely stop bothering me the way that she does?' And that is exactly what will happen. Remaining positive produces positive results. As mentioned before, we bring a lot of the bad attitudes and problems onto ourselves without even realizing it. I remember when I fed into all of the drama and created my own list of evil deeds. I never got the results that I was looking for. Also, my own world was falling in around me while I was too busy worrying about how to make another person's world fall in. Once I realized it was better to be a positive thinker, with a positive outlook, things didn't necessarily get better immediately but they most certainly stopped getting worse. When I was greeted with anger or in a mean way, I greeted back happily and with a smile. When an argument was brewing, I immediately got off of the phone or away from the scene. When negative thoughts crept into my mind I made sure to immediately replace them with a better way of thinking. I realized that I was able to control situations that way. Most importantly of all, I didn't want her to think that I was her enemy or plotting against her in any kind of way. I wanted her to feel like I wanted the best for both of us, and I really did.

No matter what, I knew it was going to be hard, but I had to practice being positive every single day. I had to make sure she only seen and heard from a positive person. This was no matter how mean, angry, or verbally abusive I was before. All of that had to be changed, and for good reason. My pride had to be set aside. I knew in the long run that she would learn to respect this 'new behavior' I had adopted much better. You won't see immediate

Soulja Soulja

results because you have to give her time to see and believe that you are really dedicated to being a better person. Some people are cool for a minute, then one disappointment they are back to being mean and rude. Just don't let her or anyone else convince you that it is better to be negative. Remember how important and valuable it is for your children to see their parents get along, without a battle. The positive person will always be the winner that winds up witnessing a mean and angry person being left no choice but to follow suit. Once you expose a negative person to positive ways it is contagious.

You may have been that person that was once negative and angry. When you said and done bad things to her and when you weren't the best boyfriend or husband that you could've been, all that you can do is become a better, more positive person from here on out and apologize. There is nothing more that you can do. There is no reason to kick yourself for the mistakes that you've made. You can't take them back but you can do much better handling the relationship that you do have, as far as parents, now and in the future. You definitely don't want to just accept that that is the way you were so that is the way you will continue to be. That will just make you an all out stupid person that will never have any good luck and keep experiencing problem after problem with your co-parent for years to come.

But something different happens when you accept that you have done wrong in the past. When you accept that you may be entertaining present nonsense and not helping to make a peaceful resolution, you are more motivated to overturn these things when they are the things that you want to be different. And once you get over your feelings of regret and ask for her forgiveness, and you sincerely apologize, then you can now let go of what was silently tearing you down. You can now move in the direction that makes sense for a peaceful future. You have lifted the weight off of your shoulders. All you need to do now is work hard at continuing to be a positive person that has his families best interest in mind at all times.

12 Gauge Shotkids

Now, whatever that she feels she needs to do to counterattack that person that you've become falls on her. When she feels that she still needs to behave rudely to satisfy her own ego she puts all of the weight on her. When she knows that she has currently, and in the past, done you wrong and she isn't apologetic about it she is hurting herself. She becomes the one that will suffer from the feelings of guilt and shame. Because over time, all that she can see is that you remain strong, encouraged, and positive. She can lie on her pillow at night and have to accept the fact that she is the only one forcing bad on the relationship that the two of you have to have. And although it is unfortunate, this is exactly what you want to happen if it has to be one person that is messing everything up. To a judge it doesn't make sense that only one person is messing everything up, but it is very much so possible. One person can be compromising and level-headed and willing to do all of the right things while the other makes a problem out of everything. They never want to agree and they have no intentions on getting along under any circumstances. They are content with being difficult. You want to be the one that is always guilt free. You don't want to have anything that she can use against you to say, 'oh you did this or that to me, so now I'm doing this and that to you.' You don't want to be the reason that she has any reason. What you continue to do to her will be the main reason why she keeps up the drama, no matter how small or large it is. The pettier it is, the better, because being petty is the best way to keep up ignorance in the first place. Ignorance thrives off of pettiness.

Overall, leave her with those problems. There is no sense in both of you being foolish. You can eliminate what you have to have on your conscience right now. You don't have to have anything further to feel sorry about later on. She will though. And it will hurt her deeper and deeper to keep on attacking and wounding a person that she can't kill, but is steady trying to. A person that is not even putting up a fight against the ignorance. This will not feel good to her for long. My favorite saying when it comes to 'baby mama drama' is that 'it is never good to fight ignorance with ignorance, because whoever is the smarter person is the loser.' Practicing that every day will relieve you greatly.

Soulja Soulja

She can't understand that so many obstacles will be in her way, and so many emotions and feelings will haunt her if she doesn't change soon. She doesn't understand that every negative action has a consequence that comes along with it. She doesn't understand how it will take a long time to mend the wounds that she is creating for her own self. Just make sure that you aren't creating your own wounds for yourself. Otherwise you can turn all of your positivity that you've displayed into being viewed negatively. When she happens to realize her mistakes you will start to see how being positive paid off for you.

9 COMFORTING THE KIDS DURING THESE TRYING TIMES

This book is intended to guide the fathers during their struggles dealing with an uncooperative co-parent. It is intended to help with controlling emotions. It is intended to help fathers understand the strategies and moves associated with an old game. But most of all it is intended to steer the focus of a distracted parent back to the most important people that have nothing to do with any changes of heart, any emotions, any problems, or anything at all; and that is the children.

While both parents, and any involved outsiders are caught up in the game and heavily focused on the effectiveness of their last plays and next strategies, the children are the ones whose emotions and well being are neglected and paid no attention. Who really cares how the children feel? The children are treated like tag-alongs that are helpless and left no choices. They are forced into situations and forced to deal with it. They are forced into the lives and care of 'new boyfriends' and 'new girlfriends.' They are the ones abruptly removed from the lives of a parent that they love more than anything in the world. They have to feel the pain of a hurt and/or angry parent that has so much steam to release that they even release it in front of their very own children without even thinking first on how that will affect them. Who even cares about how much the child loves the other parent? Children are coaxed into losing that love for that parent. Just because one parent has dislike for the other parent they encourage the children to do the same. They use this as another strategy to win over the emotions of the co-parent, or to make themselves feel better.

Forcing children to take sides and angrily discussing the child's parent is poisonous to a child, and it is downright wrong and immature. When you have an issue with a co-parent the right thing to do is to either keep it between you and that parent or to work it out on your own. You don't involve a child. Their minds are not intended to take on adult situations. Problems don't last forever between two people and they tend to get worked out eventually. But what happens when you plant that bad seed into the mind of a child? You have explained to them the problem, but never explained to them about the solution. Now all that they are trying to comprehend is problem after problem. Once you've reached the solution, you are content with that, but forgot about the bitter thoughts that you've planted in the child about their parent. These thoughts last on a child forever sometime. It is far too easy to get sidetracked by the playful spirit, the smiley faces, and the cooperativeness of a child than to recognize the effects of the brainwashing and the constant pressures that are put on them. Kids don't show this too easily because they know they can easily upset you or get themselves in trouble by voicing their concerns or opinions. They would rather not get on your bad side when they can already tell that you are down and out. So they hold in all of their feelings and just soak up and nod off on what the parent is saying to attack or degrade the other parent. Don't think for one second that this is what they want to hear though. Don't think for one second that it is what they want to feel. Don't even think for

12 Gauge Shotkids

one second that it is making their lives any better by you feeling the way that you do. It definitely isn't. I remember going through this as a ten year old child on both sides, from both parents, and all that it did was make me extremely angry and give me a headache. I hated to hear either parent talk about the other parent, and eventually that was whether it was good or bad. I hated it with a passion. In fact, to this date, I can't remember anything that made me feel any worse, even as an adult. It does something to you to hear your mother talk badly about your father. It is the same when your father says something about your mother. When they did this I couldn't help but to feel as if they were talking about me too. I was very much so apart of the very person that they were dogging, and they weren't. It couldn't have hurt them one bit to be so mean and negative toward the other parent; that wasn't their blood relative. But it beat me up badly.

What are you really intending on accomplishing by talking badly about your co-parent to a child? What is it that you expect a child to do or feel? Even talking badly about them to other people in front of the child is just as bad. You don't need children that are bought up on negative thoughts and feelings. Whatever it may be that you think they need to know they will find it out on their own one day. Talking badly just turns around and makes them start to resent you. You will look like the bad guy that is overwhelmed with hurt and hatred. No matter what the co-parent has done to you they have not made the children feel that way. They have a whole different love for their children. You will not be successful at making a child feel the pain that you do. What they feel for that parent is what they should feel on their own. All that you should be discussing with the children in regards to the co-parent is how they are feeling when they are in the care of that parent. You should be making sure that they are eating properly. You should be making sure no one is hurting them or threatening them. All that should be discussed is their well being. Other than that, you always want to listen to what the children have to say about their parent. You only want to make sure that they have happy feelings and are growing up the way children are supposed to and not having the thoughts of

Soulja Soulja

an adult because they are constantly being thrown into adult situations.

These times call for less stress and increased parenting skills. They call for more prayer. They call for more time spent on the kids. You can wrap your mind around a million and one things to do and say to their mother, but don't keep putting the kids on the back burner. Believe it or not, we can sometime become envious of our very own children because they always have the person that we silently wish that we had. It is a very secret feeling, but it does happen to be a real feeling. This may be what keeps us from enjoying time with our children like we are supposed to. Those feelings have to be burned. It is not ever going to be the children's fault as to what happened to their mother and father's relationship. You can't go about life feeling uncomfortable spending time and hanging out with your own children. They grow so fast that if you don't pay attention to them at certain stages of their growth you will miss out. If you don't talk to them or listen to them you will miss out. You will really regret that later on. We may think they stay young forever but that is so far from the truth. They grow and they tell us how they felt like outcasts, how they didn't experience a real childhood, how they don't remember having fun as a child, how they hated to visit a parent, and/or how they were lost in their own worlds.

We must acknowledge that our children feel pains and emotions due to separations as well as we do, no matter how they look. That is why this is the time to be 'superdad.' Take their minds as far away from the separation as possible. You want them to somehow feel like it isn't so bad to have mommy and daddy apart. You want them to look forward to going to daddy's house and getting a break from mama. You want this time to be more exciting at all times than it was when the two of you were together.

And this is exactly what it should be. You are loving them better and harder than you ever have before. Once upon a time you were so at ease and certain that the children would be there when you got home. You weren't worried about any separation. You could

12 Gauge Shotkids

see your children at any time and at any minute. Life was good; it was peaceful and you had none of the worries that you do now. Now you are lucky to see them twice out of the week. There is never enough time to juggle school and/or work, personal time, and still have time to spend with the kids. When you didn't have to concentrate on so much before, you have to do it all now just to stay up on game. You have to involve yourself in their schooling and their ever-changing minds now more than ever. There is just not enough time in a day anymore.

There is definitely not enough time to be worried about what their mother is doing, saying, or plotting to do. You can have ninety-nine other problems but as soon as she becomes ONE, that ONE problem will outweigh all of the other ninety-nine problems that you have. She will consume all of the mental capacity that you have and you will take away from discovering new things that you can be doing with your children. It is bad enough that they are already a splitting image of her. Now when you see them she is on your mind triple time. Don't ever let her have that kind of power over you that you can't even think straight when you should be enjoying your children. Constantly make new and exciting plans for your time with them. Make yourself look forward to the weekend, or whatever times that you have with them. This takes your mind and their minds away from any drama. Making these plans are the perfect stress reliever for you and the best way to promote a healthy, happy child. You want to make their mother see that you are a great and proud father. Try to always send the kids home overjoyed and bragging about their time away with dad. It will also make her want to step her parenting level up a notch when she sees that she isn't keeping up with doing positive and exciting things with the children. The kids will always remember the parent, or parents, that made their childhood worthwhile. Just as well as they soak up any negativity they will do the same with positivity. Instead of them later venting about how they were hurt or neglected in some kind of way they will respect the decisions that their parents made and understand how everything was done for the better for everyone.

Soulja Soulja

Don't be the weak parent. Don't be the one that is always numb and that is always talking about how bad you want their mother back. Don't be the parent that is always down in the dumps, whether you are alone or with the kids. Nobody wants to hear how bad you want your dead relationship back. The kids definitely don't need to hear it.

Although I don't think there is a child in the world that wouldn't want to have both of their parent's together, children can see when their parents don't need to be together just as well. They may rather they'd be together, but they can understand why they're separated. Especially children that have witnessed physical abuse between the two, or the ones that are always exposed to nonstop arguing. Children that have to comfort a mother that is hurt by their father coming home only when he wants to, or other obvious reasons, usually can do without mommy and daddy together. The children only want happiness between the parents, no matter if they are together or apart. But you often find the broken-hearted parent displaying their weaknesses to the children. The children don't need to witness, nor hear weakness from either parent. A weakened parent only really cares about what it is that is making him/her weak. They also only care about what they need to do to temporarily mask their problems. Now you have a parent that is obsessed with their own emotions and can't help but to abuse alcohol and drugs. They have to find a way to hurt the other parent and have no problem using the children as a weapon. They are spaced out all of the time. They can't pay attention to their children. They are losing themselves slowly but surely.

The weakness is real and will consume you if you let it. It will cause you to act out in crazy ways and say crazy things. When your children have already grown to recognize you as a brave giant in their eyes, you can immediately show them you are no more of a giant than the leader in the ant farm. A weak father will have their children asking God to bring their parents back together when that would be a disastrous thing for God to do to those poor children. A weak parent will eventually weaken their kids. They will have their children whining and blaming the other parent for making

12 Gauge Shotkids

decisions that they will later on learn was for their own well being. That actually leads to the next point.

A parent can have a weakness for the other parent, but they can also have a weakness for their own children. While we are supposed to take heed to their thoughts and opinions, because any person can learn even from a baby, you still have to know when you are making the right decisions for the well being of your future and your children's future. If it was necessary for you to leave a situation, for whatever reasons, you have to stick to it. Going back to dead or unsafe relationships for the sake of the kids can increase the trauma done to everyone in the household. The kids may be subject to a weakened parent that is making them miss the happy times, and thus making them lash out or react to you in certain strange ways at times. You must remain firm, since you are the stronger one that knows what is best. Once a separation occurs and the kids stop seeing and/or hearing the bad, they tend to think that now it is all good and it really isn't. They will think everything would be just fine if mommy and daddy got back together, but it would be the opposite. They see and hear the weakness in the weak parent and they get emotional and weak because of it.

If my mother wouldn't have remained strong she would have went back to a dead relationship over and over, just off of me and my prayers alone. God ended up knowing best in the end, despite me being encouraged to recite my young prayers to bring them back together. Instead His plan was to bless me and my mother and my siblings with the best step-father that I could have ever asked for. His plan was to bless my father with a better life and situation than he could've asked for. The problem was that I was a kid and I was always told that God would answer all of my prayers and give me whatever I wanted if I asked. No one said that He wouldn't give me what I asked for. So, being weak and asking a child to pray for something like that it could've very well made me think God was a fake for not answering my prayers. I could've had a lasting disappointment for God off of that. That is why I don't encourage parents to be weak in front of children at all. You can do all sorts of things to their little minds that will have a great affect on them

Soulja Soulja

well into adulthood. If you, as the parent, want that sort of outcome you should pray for that yourself. If you get your children into prayer have them pray that mommy and daddy stay safe and they stay happy.

Kids appreciate a parent that is responsible. They appreciate a parent that is aggressive in maintaining communication and interaction with them. They appreciate it when their father holds his end of the visitation schedule.

Make sure that you stay on top of your visitation schedule. We have all heard the stories before about the kid that was waiting on the father that never showed up. We understand how the child was greatly affected well into adulthood because of it. We saw the pain in the child's eyes. We saw as his/her mother had to comfort them and try to say things to make them feel better and take their mind off of it. We've all heard this before; some of us have experienced this for ourselves in our own lives. And the truth is that scenario happens all day every day. It happens to young children all over the world. It is definitely not something you want your children to have to experience.

In fact, as a father myself, that scenario would be a nightmare to me if I heard either one of my children reciting such a story, whether now or later in life. I never want my child to experience those feelings ever. I do understand that sometime you won't be able to make it but that has to be communicated to the child. Don't ever give your word to a child and think that it is cool to just not show up, not call, or never give an explanation. Children look forward to every single minute that you can give them. They look forward to being in your presence. They look forward to being under dad. This not only goes for regular visitation; it goes for field trips, outings, or whatever it may be that you gave them your word that you would be in attendance for. You won't believe how eager they are about it and how let down that are by it not going the way it was supposed to.

12 Gauge Shotkids

Some men seek vengeance on their co-parent, and won't spend time with the children all because they are concerned about what she is doing with her free time. They are more caught up in wanting to punish her than to produce happy children. It is not the children's fault and they deserve to have their father. Men that do this don't see that they can't hurt the mother that way, they only punish their children. Just because she can't go to the club now doesn't mean that she can't just bring the club to her. Just because she can't spend the night with her new boyfriend doesn't mean that she can't invite him over to spend the night with her. Now she is forced to bring her personal lifestyle around the children, which is exactly what most fathers don't want to happen. And she will do whatever she wants to do because she is grown and she can do that. Every negative action produces a negative reaction that will keep a person angrier instead of achieving the happiness they initially sought out. Selfishly, a man would do whatever it is that he wanted to do with his free time, but does his best to prevent the woman from having any free time. The most that he does is anger her, which in turn causes her to be more aggravated by him and have less patience when dealing with the children. How does it feel when the kids are constantly talking about how mean mom has become, or how often she is dropping them off everywhere else all of the time just so she can get away from them for a while? It sounds to me like the father's intentions actually backfired and punished his own kids instead. Because she is going to do what she wants to do regardless, and by any means.

So pick up your kids when you are supposed to. Allow their mother to have her free time just as well as you do. Neither of you would have much free time from the kids at all if you were still together, so this time could be looked at as a blessing. There are far too many kids and teenagers that go weeks and months and years without seeing their dads. Very few of them even know why. Even still, there is no excuse for a father to not be visiting with his children. I have personally experienced a co-parent that tried her best to deny me my parenting time; so off to court we go. I don't waste any time with filing petitions for contempt and getting in front of the judge. Because if they take them from you and the

Soulja Soulja

police won't get involved all you have is the courts. And every day that you go without your babies can tear your mind, body, and soul up when you know that someone is holding them from you. Demonstrating your eagerness to be with your children will end up being the force that will keep your co-parent from feeling like keeping them from you is the right move to make. They will think twice knowing that you keep documentation and will drag them in front of the judge. It's the ones that don't take the active approach, and just give up that loses at the hands of a co-parent. Also, coming and going when you want to messes everything up. You will make yourself look irresponsible and not even a judge will take you serious because you are the one that said that these times and dates were good for you, so you are expected to stick to them or change them to better times that work. Being lazy will only drag you under the rug and have your kids later attacking you about how you were never there. Because it was mentioned before that you lose out when you aren't constantly on top of the stages of growth that your children are experiencing. You miss out on tons when you just go three months without seeing them. Some fathers easily miss six months to a year with no visitation, and/or very minimal communication. All of the different changes that they experience will fall on you for not being there to help them through it. Missing the teenage years are the worst years to miss because of all of the different emotions and body changes they experience. And if you have a teenage daughter that you are missing out on, BEWARE. She is going to go for your jugular as soon as she gets brave enough to lash out at you.

Instead of all of that, constantly let your children know that you will always and forever be there to love them. Let them know you will be there to watch them grow. Let them know that you will never leave them. Even more than letting them know, make sure that this is what they can see at all times. Because children really do worry about if they are going to see you again once they have been forced to live life without you for days, weeks, or months at a time. When they have a mother that will keep them from their father at any given time they value their time with their father. And

12 Gauge Shotkids

their father should do the same because he too doesn't know when the next bomb will drop or the next battle will rage.

In heated relationships with a co-parent, make sure your children know that you will always fight for them. They need to always be comforted by the thought that you said you are coming for them no matter what. Like a hostage waiting on rescue, they can hear the bombs dropping, they don't know when but they do know that they will be rescued. And you want to stick to that word. You don't want to let them down. Since they can't fight they need you to enforce their rights as well. It will all be done too. A persistent and aggressive father won't live without his kids and if he does have to go a minute or two without them he will hold on to plenty of hope that they will return to his arms very soon. He will always keep some fight in him to show the opposition that they will never find a way to defeat him. His life depends on it, and the future of his children's minds and well being depends on it.

The reward is greater than the fight. It may seem like fathers always get the worst end of the stick, but a great father is acknowledged and respected very much. I will never forget the look in peoples' eyes when they actually see me walking in the park or shopping at the grocery store with my babies. I can't forget the respect that I receive from women/mothers that seen the pressures and the fight that I had to put up with and endure. I can never forget about the admiration that I got from other men/fathers when they can hear and see how much I adore spending precious time with my babies. Most of all, I always acknowledge being blessed enough to make a life for my family. I have been fortunate enough to keep a roof over our heads, keep the bills paid, and keep food in our mouths with very little to no struggle. It is because I learned early in life to focus on what is more important than to blow it off and dig holes all over the place that I would later have to pull myself out of. What is important will make you pay attention to how to nurture it and make it grow. Either you can act as if you don't care, or never try to learn and repeat the same cycles over and over, or you can figure out what could be going

Soulja Soulja

wrong in all areas and create a better present and future based off of what you've learned from your past.

I will always let my babies know when there is a problem and what it may be, without involving them in adult business or bad mouthing their mother. Sometime, depending on their age and mental capacity, you have to inform them of some things before they can be convinced that it is your fault that events are happening. I'm talking about when you are forced to miss visitation, blocked from communicating over the phone, forced to miss holidays, birthdays, etc. These things that a child takes to heart you may have to simply explain that 'mommy won't allow it.' It is the truth. Sadly, they will end up feeling resentment and anger for their mother, but if you don't let them know, they will have these feelings of resentment for you. And that's not right when it isn't even your fault. As long as you are there when you can and when you are supposed to be the child will see that too and take everything into consideration. You definitely don't want them growing up and holding you accountable for not doing what you were willingly and available to do. It won't change the love that they have for their mother but it will allow them to see what she is capable of doing. It will also let them know that daddy is trying, and if it were totally up to him it wouldn't be this way.

10 CONSEQUENCES FOR THE 'BAD PARENT'

Mothers and fathers both have to understand what a difficult job it is to raise children. They have to realize that although it can be very difficult they have to learn to get along and partner up with their co-parent. It is a tedious job to be able to control your feelings and emotions and be able to compromise with the co-parent to make decisions that will benefit your children. Those people that are just so interested in having their own little bundle of joy will quickly realize that that bundle of joy will affect their lives in several different areas as well as the lives of many others. They will realize that the bundle of joy is not quite 'all theirs' to begin with. You don't create them alone nor will you be alone in raising them and making decisions on their well being. Any parent that thinks that 'this is my child' subjects themselves to major backlash when dealing with a caring, concerned, and loving co-parent. They set their minds up to learn to play unusual games with the child and the co-parent in the near future. They deny their child the full

Soulja Soulja

love that they are supposed to be experiencing from the 'village' that it takes to raise them. Blindly, they set themselves up for payback in the present and the future due to the actions and games they've played in the past.

There are many, many consequences for bad parenting that often go unrecognized. Mothers and fathers just go through their struggles without realizing why things are going so terribly. Eventually they learn to accept their lives going the way they are going. Mothers who play games with their co-parent for years don't even realize that they are the main and initial reason that they've become single mothers in the first place. She thought it was all fun and games to hurt a father by taking his children away from him until he just stopped fighting altogether, went out and made another family, and left her to fend for herself. She didn't think that there was anything wrong with making a potentially great father look bad in front of a judge and other outsiders to the relationship. She thought it was cool to deny him his visitations, until he stopped showing up completely. She thought that it was cool to be like her lonely, single mother friends and family that brag about how they are 'mama' and 'daddy,' and how they have to do everything on their own. This is the life that she wanted to experience so she started playing games with her co-parent and her children. She thought it was cool to say 'my baby daddy is a deadbeat.'

She clearly missed telling the world what she did initially to stimulate all of the negative feelings and force the absence of the father. She clearly don't want to talk about how she pushed him all of the way to his limits. She fails to mention how she made him feel unwanted, turned his children away from him, threw dirt on his name, took his money and denied him parenting time, etc. She only wants to show the world what the aftermath is but not how the war began. This is because she is now getting what she asked for initially while she was conspiring her every game strategy, and now she has no one left to play with. The games have been over and now the prize for winning isn't what she needed it to be. She needs help now because kids grow up. They talk more, they think

12 Gauge Shotkids

more, they feel more, they eat more, and they consume more of everything. It's not as easy as it was when they were under ten years of age. It would be nice now if their daddy were there to relieve her of her struggles and stresses a little bit.

This is what they eventually face. And I don't condone nor encourage any fathers to walk out on their families at any point, for any reason. I encourage them to stay and fight until things start looking up but this scenario is our reality in the world. Every father isn't a fighter. Some men know if they take anymore nonsense they may seriously hurt you, so they get out of the way. Some men don't know how to keep up a fight so they give up somewhere in the midst of the battle. Even while dealing with the courts it has never been designed for a father to win. This is why it takes so long to see justice, if any at all. A father that can't take anymore will simply leave the family altogether, and most will never return. Now years later you get this mother coming out of nowhere ranting and raving about how hard she has it. This isn't the case all of the time in the households but it would be completely wrong to not acknowledge that mothers can force themselves into single parenthood by mimicking the actions and the lifestyles of other mothers around the world with the same mind to hurt a father by using their children as weapons.

What happens to these children though? Do they develop normally? Do they live normal lives? I won't say that the children can't grow normally but they do experience more difficulties than children in the average loving and two parent households. And why wouldn't they? They had to grow up with two parents arguing back and forth, couldn't ever get along, and they sometimes get caught up in the middle of the drama. They had to grow up either not seeing their father, or barely seeing him, and only at the mother's discretion. Those that didn't get to see their father at all have to grow up wondering why. Was it mama's fault that daddy wasn't around, or did daddy just stop coming around?

Now we have a population of kids that are lost and confused. Some of them have a hard time focusing in school. They are so distracted

Soulja Soulja

by what is going on at home that they start dropping grades or not caring about school altogether. They grow to be rebellious against the parent that caused them the most hurt. Especially the one that spoke so negatively of the other parent or forced the other parent out of the kid's lives. This happens to be a consequence even if you are the single parent that has busted your butt to make a living for the family. If you caused them pain, no matter how much you are trying to do right, they will still rebel on you. There is no getting away from this. Just when you thought they didn't know or that they were too young, you had no idea how much they were taking in and storing up. Now it's time to pay and you can't blame them.

When you subject children to the negative images, lifestyles, and languages of a 'disturbed home,' you raise their chances of having extreme attitude and behavior problems. They've been so used to hearing negativity and soaking it up that they end up releasing it the same way they received it. It's hard to blame them; their first teachers taught this to them. You have boys that are eager to fight girls and girls that are eager to provoke boys to fight them. You have boys and girls that have racing minds that can't wait to get involved with each other. They are so used to witnessing male and female interaction on an adult level that now they think that they are fast enough to think and act like adults. Now you have kids that don't know how to be kids anymore, even at very young ages. This increases the pregnancy rate for our teenage girls and it increases the crime rate for our boys that are eager to impress the boys and the girls with their adult-like activity.

When a parent has been absent from a child's life that child doesn't fully learn why they think and act the way that they do. They grow up but don't understand themselves thoroughly. They have a hard time figuring out why they have certain habits or why they feel certain ways that they don't notice from the other side of the family. Most times if they are missing a parent they also miss out on that parent's complete side of the family. They don't interact with their grandparents, aunts, uncles, or cousins from that side. How could this be a normal way of living? The only reason that they don't complain is because this is the only way that they've

12 Gauge Shotkids

learned to live. But it most definitely should not be looked at as normal.

And who really is thinking about how messed up their kids may turn out to be as a result of their current actions? No one is worried about how important it is going to be for that child to have the wisdom and training from that particular mother and father. They don't know what or who that child is going to grow up to be or need. They don't think about how they are stunting the growth of that child's future. They don't care while they are too busy thinking about themselves.

Due to the high rate of single family homes and lack of fathers our children have become worse. Not only that, overall parenting has become worse. More parents are paying less attention to the kids and they are letting them get away with all kinds of things. Just from simply playing games with a co-parent to get a reaction, kids are growing up and going to prison and jails, they are rebellious to their parents, they are dropping out of school, and doing all sorts of drugs and substance abusing. They aren't going down the right streets because they were bought up all wrong. Then you have parents who want to cry about it because they wind up being the ones paying for all of it right along with the child, but all along they were the ones who were more focused on themselves more than teaching their kids better. Now they are stuck running in and out of courthouses, paying debts bought on by the children, trying to keep boys from running through their daughters, and dealing with out of control mouths and behaviors. It is all a part of their consequences that they've bought on themselves.

Kids that have been damaged adults; they become the adults that are left behind all of the productive and educated adults. They are the ones that have a harder time becoming and remaining stable throughout their young adult life, especially in their twenties. It's harder for them to shake the trauma that they've experienced in their past, dealing with no father and an unstable mother who tried to do the best that she could on her own. The kids remain very dependent at times and most never really grasp the real

Soulja Soulja

fundamentals of life due to the fact that they weren't taught that way. The fundamentals that I mean are the ones that deal with creating a family, raising a family, and staying together. They don't learn the importance of being responsible; keeping a job, paying bills on time, furthering their education and skills, owning a home, and maintaining a loving family. They never saw these ways of living so they never used their minds to venture in those directions. This isn't the full reality with all households and families at all, but a great majority of them came from poverty just to raise their own families in poverty. You will rarely hear about their sophisticated goals or see them make plans for the future that they are actually living to accomplish. Even those in their late twenties that have gained some insight on better living situations find that they have just drug themselves so far in the mud, possibly from drinking, drugging, and partying so much that they are now paying for past mistakes that constantly hold them back. Some just say forget it and keep living the way that they've been living and just accepting their lives the way that they are.

The parents that bought on this mentality don't really get the chance to live the most fulfilling lives either. They have dug themselves so deep of a hole and either attempted to climb out of it with very little to no success or they have learned to simply rest in it. As mentioned before, mothers who damage the mentalities and lives of their children live their lives suffering financially and dealing with the consequences of their own children's mistakes. They run themselves raggedy by having to involve themselves so deeply in the mess that hard-headed, smart-mouthed, uncontrollable teenagers put them in. Even when the children are grown adults the parents have to deal with the mistakes from the monsters they've created.

When you see the middle aged and older people forced to go crazy over their kids that have turned into irresponsible and problem-ridden adults, these are usually the ones that have messed up with their kids while they were young. In turn, they have problems, because when you do wrong you have to pay. You start to see many older men who can't even talk to their children without the

12 Gauge Shotkids

conversation turning into an argument. Their daughters that don't want to have anything to do with them will not even let them have interaction with their own kids. Therefore they lack a decent relationship with their grandchildren. Men have to be very cautious of what they expose their daughters to, because while she is grown, and her and her father have little to no communication, she could be receiving the same abuse from the males in her life that her mother may have received from men in the past. Instead of feeling comfortable communicating this to her father, she has no intention on filling him in on her reality. She winds up suffering the same way her mother may have. This would be a pain to any father to know his daughter is being abused in any way.

Also, parents wonder why they can't live the dreams that they once dreamed before. They wonder why they still live at a poverty level. They wonder how they are so grown and yet still so dependent. They also wonder if they will ever see better days. Although they will continue to be blessed by God and have what they need to survive, their past will limit them on how big their blessings are until they have made up for their wrongs. And some parents will still refuse to accept their wrongdoings, or even continue to do them with their younger children, so they continue to fall short. They will also be subject to further attack by those younger ones once they get old enough. What can you really do or say to them when they don't even know or care about what they are doing to hurt their children, but you sit back and watch them have breakdown after breakdown? They can't remain stable so they move house to house. They struggle off and on to keep food, to keep decent transportation, to keep a decent job, and simply to live altogether. It is harder for them to live an average life. They spend more time catching cases and landing in jails and prisons. Numerous downfalls creep up to affect the lives of those that don't repent for their wrongs. And it's even uglier when you have spent your life not caring about what you do wrong to other people (your co-parent and your kids) and then once your life turns upside-down when all the games are over no one even really seems to care how you're managing.

Soulja Soulja

Life just does not get right. It can't seem to get better. When you get two steps ahead, you get knocked back down three steps. You will wonder why. All that you will have to do is sit back and reflect though. You can see that the kids have experienced so much in their young lives that they have carried a lot of it into their adult lives. You can see that they have become adults that are irresponsible, that take advantage, cut corners, and are abusive. You can see your own ways reflecting off of them. You can see that they blame you and resent you when they make mistakes.

All of this should show you that it is time to take action and try to make things right. You can start by accepting that you have done wrong. You can explain those wrongs to the children. Instead of letting the trauma pass to another generation, you can start shifting what they may think is right into something they know is not healthy for adults, because you can prove it. Use your own experiences as examples where they can see how it has affected you. Because it doesn't really pay to say something is a problem without being able to show how it affects a person. This is how people learn. At least if you can recognize why your life is going the way that it is and you're apologetic and trying to encourage change before it destroys more lives, you can switch up your own reality into a much better life. This is the perfect way of showing and having an effect. If your children grew to always see you having issue after issue, without recognizing or hearing why you have these issues, they too may experience the same issues and not understand or try to even see why. This is how you create generations of people doing the same things repetitively.

Without shaping up you put yourself at risk of your kids turning on you later on in life. This has to be terrible to have you own flesh and blood not care about anything that you stand for or care to listen to anything you have to say. But kids do suffer heavy damage from a parent dogging or mistreating another parent throughout their lives. Mothers tend to think they will have their kid's respect forever, no matter what. Then they do and say anything they choose to the children. They think that they can just make them feel however that they want them to feel and the kids

12 Gauge Shotkids

just have to take it. But eventually they do the exact opposite. They will lose respect for her if she isn't giving them the proper respect. Some kids grow to be so bold that they will feel no shame or fear in attacking or cursing their own mother. Girls usually take more from their mothers but will turn on their fathers quicker. Boys will turn on their mothers for disrespecting them and they are quicker to become distant from them.

It never can be satisfying to not have a healthy relationship with your child no matter how old they are or what they've done. And when parent and child fall apart, they either come back together pretty fast and build a better bond or they don't speak for very long periods of time due to their pride and similar attitudes. But there really are parents that have dragged their children through the mud. They have cursed them all through their lives. They have forced them to believe that they are worthless or aren't beautiful, just like their other parent (in all of the worse ways), or they are bad children. They did and said all of these things but they still demand respect. The old sayings about how the parent can do or say anything that they want to their children because they raised them, sheltered them, and fed them are so overrated and misstated. They will actually bring problems to a parent in the future. Although you deserve the utmost respect for being a parent that provides, that doesn't give you the right to be disrespectful and/or treat your children any kind of way that you see fit. It will backfire on you later when you see how they really turn out from your upbringing.

Kids didn't ask to be here. So if you bought them here, YOU, and not them took on that responsibility to clothe them, feed them, shelter them, and prepare them to fend for themselves. You can't blame them for what you are supposed to be doing anyway. You bought that on yourself to make sacrifices for their well being. They shouldn't be talked to all crazy or mistreated just because you have to do all of this and that for them. This will make them turn on you when they are old enough to understand. You can also make a child feel like they are a burden to you. Also, making them feel like they are a problem because they have characteristics like the other parent is your fault as well. That is the person that you chose to have children with. Naturally, due to genetics this is what happens; a child will display very similar looks, behaviors, and characteristics as both of their parents. Don't feel bad though, they most likely have an equal amount of you in them as well. You may just choose to want to pay attention to what bothers you the most about the other parent. No matter what, they didn't ask to be here and it is not their fault that they're here.

Beware. Every action has a reaction. Make sure that before you plant your seeds that you have an idea of what you are going to grow. Make sure that you know who the real victims are while you are plotting and committing household crimes. The victim that you are really focused on just may not be the only victim that you are affecting.

Probably the most overlooked part of all of the drama that no one seems to ever worry about is the way that they are affecting the partnership that they have with the co-parent. While everyone is angry and battling, they don't stop to think about how it probably shouldn't be so easy to hurt a relationship with a person that no matter what they still have to know and interact with at various points and times throughout life.

Back about fifty or sixty years ago, various programs were introduced to American households that were designed to help feed, clothe, and shelter families. They were put into place by our government and some still remain today. These programs include SNAP (Supplemental Nutrition Assistance Program), housing assistance (Section 8 or Housing), and W.I.C. (Women, Infant, Children). These programs were easy to apply for but there were a few catches in order to qualify for them. One catch was you had to have an income that was below poverty level. Another catch was that there couldn't be a working father in the household. I repeat......there could not be a working father in the household.

This eliminated the father, involved the government, and forced the mothers to want to live at poverty levels just to get all of this free assistance. They could get food (and lots of it), a home (and a

12 Gauge Shotkids

nice one), and milk and various nutritional foods for their infants and toddlers for little or nothing at all. All that they had to do was raise the family without the father. They didn't have to worry about working. They didn't have to be under the control of a breadwinner anymore. They had somewhat gained a freedom and an independence if that's what you want to call it. After all of the years of having to live off of a man, they no longer needed a man to survive.

But was this all for the better or did it make matters worse? Surely I don't believe that either program was intended to live off of for long or forever. But they have been. I don't believe that it was intended for women to get lazy and arrogant and turn on the fathers of their children; some have even removed the father from the children's lives completely. But they have. It seems that the programs were openly welcomed and abused and it opened the leader's eyes to the society of beasts they could create. It showed them how dependent poverty-stricken folks could be. It showed how much they would now have available to spend with the money they hustled up on consumer items to make the rich richer. That's why we have so much more available to buy now, and it's mostly advertised to poor people. Poor people are the largest consumers of items that aren't needed for survival. You would think that all that they would be purchasing is enough to survive. But that isn't the case, and they were able to see that early on. Because if you fast forward, you have a super high rate of single family homes with mothers also proud to claim the role of 'dad' as well. And a mother could never be a dad. She will never have it in her to be one. But she has benefits and assistance though. You have very high unemployment rates amongst poverty-stricken households. You have high crime rates, with the most crimes being committed by the poorest people. And you have so many deadbeat dads that find it far too easy to just walk out on their families. Everyone would rather be single and collect government benefits than to raise and nurture prosperous families where you have an active mother and father in the household with all intentions on growing together. You think they are just giving these benefits out without getting back in more ways than you could think of? If so, then why aren't they broke by doing so? They are profiting off of our ignorance toward ourselves and each other.

When will we realize that our partnerships with our co-parents are the difference between our children being raised to be strong or wrong? When will we learn to respect our lives, our children, and our co-parents enough by at least being the smarter, more responsible parent and acknowledging that we need our co-parent to be at their best and an overall great partner? We don't do our children any justice by beefing and having drama with our co-parents. The more that we hurt the co-parent, the more we weaken any chance of having a strong partnership in the future. A partnership where we can openly discuss our children together, we can be proud of our children together, we can love our children together, whether we are in a relationship or not, and we can raise our children to be prosperous, strong individuals.

This may be a task at its earlier stages, but it should not be a hard decision made too tough to stomach as time goes by and both parents realize they will never be back together and in love. For the sake of the children don't stay in a relationship, but stay together. Lord knows that no child wants to grow to be an adult and still see that their parents still despise one another and can't get along. Or maybe they've warred so hard during their breakup that they now live in a silent, shame-filled shell. Every child deserves to have decent parents that are perfect to them and for them. Forget 'babymama' and 'babydaddy' for one moment and realize that you are a parent and a co-parent.......and NO CHILD DESERVES THE DRAMA!

ABOUT THE AUTHOR

Soulja Soulja was born Rodney L. Clark in 1984. He is the creator of RapSpire Music, born in 2009. RapSpire is a positive and inspirational brand of rap music that is designed to uplift and motivate the listeners to do better in their lives and stay motivated on the purposes for their lives no matter what obstacles get in the way.

Soulja Soulja is an Indiana native that actively performs RapSpire music, poetry, and guest speaking. He has three children that he loves and cares for deeply. He is also the oldest child of nine children. He has three brothers and five sisters.

Soulja Soulja has been writing and recording music and poetry for thirteen years to date. He has released two studio albums that are available on iTunes, and a host of mixtapes that are currently available for download. Just search 'rapspire' anywhere on the internet for more information, music downloads, music videos, poetry, and contact information.

Soulja Soulja has published another book titled 'Young: And Having Faith N The Hood' in late 2014. It is available now on Amazon, Barnes and Noble, and other various book retailers. More releases to come in 2016 and 2017.

Stay tuned in for much more from Soulja Soulja, R3D Books, and RapSpire Music Group.

RapSpire is the movement!

www.ingramcontent.com/pod-product-compliance
Lightning Source LLC
Chambersburg PA
CBHW031256110426
42743CB00039B/519